ASIAN AMERICAN AUTHORS

The *Collective Biographies* Series

Collective Biographies

ASIAN AMERICAN AUTHORS

Kathy Ishizuka

Enslow Publishers, Inc.

40 Industrial Road   PO Box 38
Box 398   Aldershot
Berkeley Heights, NJ 07922   Hants GU12 6BP
USA   UK

http://www.enslow.com

To my mother, who instilled in me the love of books

Library of Congress Cataloging-in-Publication Data

Ishizuka, Kathy.
    Asian-American authors / Kathy Ishizuka.
        p. cm. — (Collective biographies)
    Profiles the lives of ten famous Asian-American writers, including Carlos
Bulosan, Sook Nyul Choi, Maxine Hong Kingston, Marie G. Lee, Bette Bao
Lord, Kyoko Mori, Bharati Mukherjee, Amy Tan, Yoshiko Uchida, and
Laurence Yep.
    Includes bibliographical references and index.
    ISBN 0-7660-1376-6
    1. Asian American authors—Biography—Juvenile literature. 2. Authors,
American—20th century—Biography—Juvenile literature. [1. Authors,
American. 2. Asian Americans—Biography.] I. Title. II. Series.
PS153.A84 I84 2000
810.9'895 – dc21
                                   99-051005

Printed in the United States of America

10 9 8 7 6 5 4 3 2 1

To Our Readers:
All Internet addresses in this book were active and appropriate when we went to press.
Any comments or suggestions can be sent by e-mail to Comments@enslow.com or to
the address on the back cover.

Every effort has been made to locate all copyright holders of material used in this
book. If any errors or omissions have occurred, corrections will be made in future
editions of this book.

Contents

Acknowledgment

Thank you to the authors profiled who so generously provided additional information and photographs, as well as their support to this project.

Preface

"So why do I write?" said Amy Tan. "Because my childhood disturbed me, pained me, made me ask foolish questions. . . ."[1]

All the authors in this book have engaged in a similar process. Trying to come to terms with their lives led them to write. As Laurence Yep said, while forming his book *Dragonwings,* "I was also giving form to myself."[2]

All the writers in this book share an Asian heritage—their ethnic backgrounds are Chinese, Japanese, East Indian, Filipino, and Korean—but they are as different as individuals can be. Bharati Mukherjee came from the most privileged class in India; Carlos Bulosan was born into abject poverty in the Philippines. Born and bred in the suburbs of Minnesota, Marie G. Lee grew up an all-American girl. Bette Bao Lord did not speak a word of English until she found herself in a New York classroom at the age of eight.

From such diverse backgrounds, each author, in sorting out his or her own emotions, dreams, and fears, discovered an outlet in writing.

For some, pivotal events had a profound effect upon their lives and later influenced their work. For Kyoko Mori it was the sudden loss of her mother to suicide, which she describes in both her novel

Shizuko's Daughter and her painful memoir *The Dream of Water*. When she was just a teenager, Amy Tan was devastated by the deaths of both her brother and her father, and later by the violent death of a close friend.

"Everyone wonders about the roads not taken," recalled Bette Bao Lord. "Only we immigrants can point to the fork that above all else has shaped our destinies."[3] Half the authors in this book began their lives anew when they arrived in America. Some have written directly about those experiences, and others have shaped stories from this unique perspective. While writing her novel *The Tiger's Daughter*, Mukherjee described herself as "like a bridge, poised between two worlds."[4]

Still other lives were caught up in the sweep of history. Yoshiko Uchida was a college student when she and her family were forcibly removed from their Berkeley, California, home, during the World War II incarceration of Japanese Americans. In her novel *Year of Impossible Goodbyes*, Sook Nyul Choi fictionalizes her own daring escape to freedom after the Japanese occupation of her North Korea homeland. Bette Bao Lord was an eyewitness to the 1989 freedom demonstrations in Tiananmen Square, Beijing, China, and was inspired to describe the effect on Chinese lives in her book *Legacies*.

Perhaps less dramatic, but no less influential, is the impact of each writer's childhood. Both California natives, Laurence Yep and Maxine Hong

Kingston grew up between two cultures. Torn between her American culture and the Chinese influence of her mother's powerful talk-stories, Kingston tries to make sense of it all in her autobiographical novel *The Woman Warrior.* Growing up the only Chinese kid in a black neighborhood, Yep struggled for years to find himself. In his popular books, Yep fashions characters who are also outsiders making their own adventurous journeys of self-discovery.

From early on, all the authors fell in love with books and reading. Uchida was surrounded by books in her family's home. Sook Nyul Choi has vividly recalled "the feel and the smell of books" and "the sound of pages turning."[5] In her crowded household, Mukherjee sought refuge in books and would often find a safe corner in which to read. The library was a treasured store of knowledge for the poor and ailing Bulosan.

Love of the written word led naturally into writing. This, too, is remembered by the authors. "I was in fourth grade and all of a sudden this poem started coming out of me," wrote Kingston.[6] Marie G. Lee caught the writing bug when she got her first typewriter "and I saw how cool the words looked when they were typed," she said.[7]

Many have extended beyond their personal careers to serve the community. Bette Bao Lord campaigns actively for human rights. In addition to writing books, Marie G. Lee finds the time to participate in important causes, such as fighting anti-Asian violence and creating forums for emerging Asian American writers. In their speaking engagements, Sook Nyul Choi and Yoshiko Uchida hoped to instill in young people the lessons of history.

While the writing careers of these authors may have been sparked by deeply personal reasons, the end result is a wonderful literary legacy for us all. Reading their works will inspire a range of emotion— joy, sadness, anger, laughter, and, ultimately, triumph of the human spirit.

The connection between reader and writer completes the circle. In the words of Amy Tan:

> Writing for me is an act of faith, a hope that I will discover what I mean by "truth." And if the writer and the reader discover the same thing . . . the act of faith has resulted in an act of magic. To me, that's the mystery and the wonder of both life and fiction—the connection between two individuals who discover in the end that they are more the same than they are different.[8]

Carlos Bulosan

(1911–1956)

On a windswept hilltop in Seattle, grade-school children gather at the gravesite of Carlos Bulosan. The inscription etched on his headstone reads simply: WRITER. POET. ACTIVIST.

Once a prominent figure whose face appeared on the cover of a national magazine, Bulosan died a forgotten man in 1956, his life's work fading into obscurity.

Then, in the 1970s, Bulosan and his work were rediscovered. With his 1946 book *America Is in the Heart* now a widely read classic, Carlos Bulosan is remembered as an early pioneer in Asian American history and literature.

Carlos Bulosan

Carlos Bulosan was born November 2, 1911, in the village of Binalonan on the island of Luzon in the Philippines. To support their large family, his father farmed a small piece of land, and his mother sold vegetables and salted fish in the village. As the youngest son, Carlos was obligated to help his mother, who nurtured an adventurous spirit in her son.

Like many Filipinos at that time, the Bulosan boys dreamed of a brighter future in America. Aurelio, Carlos's elder brother, was the first to make the journey to San Francisco, in 1929. Soon another brother, Dionisio, followed. Despite Aurelio's advice to stay and finish high school, Carlos was determined to join them.

As they had done for his brothers, Carlos's parents sold a portion of their land to raise the $75 for Carlos's passage to America. So in 1930, at age nineteen, Carlos docked in Seattle, Washington, with just twenty cents in his pocket, but his spirit full of hope.

From Seattle he traveled south to Lompoc, California, to join his brother Dionisio. It was there that Carlos learned the harsh realities of Filipino life in the United States. In the difficult years of the Great Depression, the national economy collapsed and millions of Americans lost their jobs. Filipino workers, or "pinoys," suffered severe unemployment and discriminatory labor laws. Racial hatred flared into violence—Filipinos were attacked in towns all along the West Coast, from California to Washington State.

Carlos witnessed beatings and shootings. He read angry editorials calling for the segregation of Filipinos and heard threats to Filipino workers who sought fair wages. "All these happenings . . . must have jolted Carlos' sensibilities and struck deep terror in his heart," said his friend P. C. Morrante.[1] The ugly side of America angered Carlos and inspired a passionate sense of purpose that later found expression in his writing.

Meanwhile, Carlos washed dishes in a café and did other odd jobs, but his frail body and poor health made it difficult for him to work. He soon departed for Los Angeles to stay with Aurelio. A restaurant worker, Aurelio supported Carlos, who spent his time in the public library.

The library provided a welcome refuge for many unemployed people during the Depression. But for Carlos it offered the precious gift of knowledge. "From day to day I read, and reading widened my mental horizon . . . ," he wrote. "I plunged into books, boring through the earth's core, leveling all seas and oceans, swimming in the constellation."[2] He read everything from children's books to literary magazines. Reading improved his English and inspired him to write.

Aurelio gave Carlos money for a typewriter—the first of many. Always short of money, Carlos would often sell his typewriters for cash. "I always knew when he was broke," remembered Aurelio. "He would go through my wallet and put a small note back that said, 'minus twenty dollars.'"[3]

After spending his days in the library, Carlos waited to leave until the darkness of night would hide his dirty clothes. Then he walked along the streets, moving among the working people. He observed their way of life and also the hardships they faced. Many of their experiences appeared in his book *America Is in the Heart.*

Bulosan hitched rides on passing freight trains and visited the pinoys working in the fields. They were following the harvest from southern California to Washington State. In his travels, Bulosan met union leader Chris Mensalvas, who would influence the next turn in his life.

To improve working conditions, Mensalvas dedicated his life to organizing labor unions for Filipino workers, who were barred from other unions. Bulosan joined the labor movement and helped found the United Cannery and Packing House Workers of America. "Writing was not sufficient," he later wrote. "The most decisive move that the writer could make was to take his stand with the worker."[4]

In 1934, Bulosan became editor of *The New Tide,* a magazine for workers. When the first issue came off the presses, Chris and Carlos took a hundred copies and distributed them to farm workers. Although the magazine went out of existence, the

Carlos Bulosan arrived in America full of hope, which he maintained despite his difficult life.

spirit of the early Filipino leaders survived to inspire future social change.

The New Tide brought Carlos Bulosan into contact with influential writers, including William Carlos Williams and Richard Wright. He also met editor Harriet Monroe, who was the first to champion Bulosan's writing.

In 1936, Bulosan entered Los Angeles General Hospital suffering from tuberculosis, a serious disease that attacks the lungs. While he was ill, Bulosan was befriended by two sisters, Sanora and Dorothy Babb. The Babbs encouraged Carlos's efforts to educate himself, supplying him with a variety of books. During his two years of recovery, Bulosan read a book a day. "I had the opportunity to seriously read books which opened all my world of intellectual possibilities—and a grand dream of bettering society for the working man," he said.[5]

Carlos fell in love with Dorothy, but he was well aware of the pressures against interracial relationships. After they went out one evening, Carlos expressed his frustration in a letter to Dorothy: "The people were staring at us because we dared to walk down the street together. I walked home in a nightmare. But what could I say?"[6]

Despite his deep commitment and faith in his work, Carlos felt like an outcast. "Do you know what a Filipino feels in America?" he wrote in a letter. "He is the loneliest thing on earth."[7]

As the Depression lifted, Carlos Bulosan began to experience some success as a writer. In 1942, he published two volumes of poetry, *Letter from America* and *Chorus for America*. That same year he was included in the prestigious *Who's Who in America*.

Carlos's success occurred as the United States entered World War II, which brought a change in attitude toward Filipinos. Viewed as loyal allies against Japan, Filipinos were suddenly "in style."

In 1943, the *Saturday Evening Post* published artist Norman Rockwell's illustrations of the four freedoms defined by President Roosevelt: Freedom of Speech, Freedom to Worship, Freedom from Want, and Freedom from Fear. It was decided that the essay for Freedom from Want should come from someone who had known physical want. Bulosan was chosen to write the piece.

Despite these successes, Bulosan soon ran out of money. "Always my impetus to write was stronger when my financial predicaments were most embarrassing."[8] In the back of a farm-labor employment office, he would write three or four articles a day. The room was so cold that he wore an overcoat and gloves while he worked, often jumping up and down to stay warm. *The New Yorker* magazine started to buy his stories, and other sales followed. Soon after, he attracted the interest of publishers—Harcourt, Brace and Company sent him a telegram, requesting to see a manuscript.

In the spring of 1944, Harcourt, Brace published *The Laughter of My Father*, a collection of stories. It was a major success, translated into several languages and broadcast to the United States armed forces during World War II to encourage sympathy for U.S. allies in the Pacific.

The story of his father's often creative struggles to sustain his family, *Laughter* was misunderstood by critics, who found it humorous. This angered Bulosan, who said he wrote the book, not in laughter, but in tears.[9] Carlos Bulosan determined that with his next book, readers would clearly understand the Filipino experience.

Published in 1946, *America Is in the Heart* is an unflinching first-person account of Filipino American life during the Depression. The narrator arrives in America, full of dreams. But they are soon diminished. Moving among workers of all minorities—blacks, American Indians, Koreans, Mexicans—the narrator witnesses murders and lynchings and is himself beaten and driven out of various towns. Through his despair, he manages to preserve his faith in America.

One reviewer urged people to read the book, believing it would arouse such anger as "to bring to an end the vicious nonsense of racism."[10] *Look* magazine called *America Is in the Heart* one of the fifty most important American books ever published.

In 1950, Bulosan began to write again for the union. However, a widespread fear of communism during this time put union leaders under suspicion.

Because of his radical politics, Carlos Bulosan was targeted by the FBI and scheduled for deportation as a threat to national security.[11] Bulosan was also blacklisted in Hollywood, which meant no one would hire him as a writer.

In his final years, Bulosan was impoverished, stricken by despair, and virtually forgotten as a writer. His frail health was further weakened by heavy drinking. Bulosan contracted pneumonia and collapsed on the street. He died on September 11, 1956.

In 1986, friends and admirers rededicated Bulosan's gravesite at Seattle's Mount Pleasant Cemetery, erecting a proper headstone to replace the pauper's marker that was faded by the elements.

Sook Nyul Choi
(1937–   )

After being separated from their family, a ten-year-old girl takes her younger brother by the hand and they flee their war-torn country. Barefoot and bleeding, digging under barbed wire, the children make a harrowing escape across the border to freedom.

This is not fiction. Author Sook Nyul Choi was that courageous little girl, and this incredible story actually happened.

Years would pass before Choi would have the opportunity to tell her story. After becoming an American citizen, teaching for twenty years, running a business, and raising a family, Choi sat down to recall the painful memories of her childhood. With

Sook Nyul Choi

her moving autobiographical novel, *Year of Impossible Goodbyes,* Sook Nyul Choi realized her dream of becoming an author, and her story touched thousands of readers.

On January 10, 1937, Sook Nyul Choi was born in Pyongyang, North Korea. From an early age, she loved to read. "I loved the feel and the smell of books; I liked the sound of pages turning," said Choi.[1] She recalled sitting for hours under a trellis of grapevines in her backyard, reading as she snacked on bitter green grapes. "Through books, I could travel to the far corners of the world and meet people from distant lands and cultures," said Choi. "I could even travel through time."[2]

But troubled times prevented Choi from enjoying much of a normal childhood. From 1910 to 1945, Japanese soldiers occupied Korea, and in this period the Korean people suffered brutal oppression.

Choi's father and grandfather were both scholars who taught Korean history and literature. Teaching was considered an offense by the Japanese, and the two were imprisoned and tortured. Also imprisoned were Choi's three older brothers, who spent years in hard labor. With the family torn apart, Choi's mother had to to run a small factory, making socks for the Japanese army.

The Japanese were forced out of Korea after World War II. The country was then divided into two zones of occupation, with Soviet troops north and the Americans south. The cruelties continued under Soviet Communist rule, causing the ten-year-old Choi to flee North Korea with her younger brother. Alone, the two children made a daring escape across the border—the 38th Parallel—to freedom in the South.

The two reunited with their father and brothers in Seoul. Six months later, after her own escape, their mother joined them. Choi spent the next two and a half years as a refugee in Pusan, South Korea.

During this time, Choi began to write. Though just a middle-school student, she had already witnessed much suffering and death. Haunted by these memories and thoughts of loved ones left behind in North Korea, Choi found comfort in writing. "In an empty room with a pen and a small blank notebook," wrote Choi, "I felt as if I were confiding in a very special friend who understood me perfectly."[3]

Her earliest published work appeared in Korean newspapers. Decades would pass before she would write again.

Growing up in war-torn Korea, Choi was distinctly aware of foreign nations. During high school, she was taught English and French, which she studied avidly. "I developed a growing curiosity about what life was like beyond my country, and had a particular fascination with the United States," said Choi.[4]

In 1958, Sook Nyul Choi emigrated from Korea to America and enrolled in Manhattanville College in New York. She immersed herself in Western culture, from Longfellow's poetry to the Girl Scouts, which she joined as a college student.

Having to communicate only in English, however, was a challenge. For the first two years, said Choi, "my Korean-English/English-Korean dictionary never left my hands."[5] But despite the difficulties, she enjoyed her college years. Majoring in European history, French, and art, she earned a bachelor's degree.

Immediately after graduation, Choi became a U.S. citizen and began teaching at a Catholic elementary school in New York City. She married a Korean businessman, and the couple had two daughters, Kathleen and Audrey.

Meanwhile, Choi continued her career, teaching all grades in the New York City public schools, from kindergarten through high school. Choi found her work very rewarding. Responding to her students' enthusiasm for Asian culture, she incorporated Asian subjects into her curriculum. When her students requested books about Korean history, Choi was dismayed to find that little material existed. "I often wished I could write a book of my experiences growing up in Korea," said Choi. "But my teaching career and raising a family left me little time to ponder writing."[6]

After the sudden death of her husband in 1980, Choi's life was thrown into turmoil. Forced to leave teaching, she struggled to run his import-export business while raising her two young children.

During a 1981 trip to her homeland, Choi decided the time was right to tell her story. Initially, her family found it too painful. When she asked her father about some of his experiences in jail, he said, "Why do you want me to bring back the devils long gone? Why do you want to make people cry?"[7]

But it was in the spirit of her grandfather that Choi set out to write her first book. "He used to tell me that to be at peace, one had to open one's heart and be kind, accepting and forgiving of others," she wrote. "My grandfather had so many of his loved ones killed by the Japanese, and yet, he never seemed bitter."[8] Despite her own painful memories, Choi felt it was important to reveal this little-known chapter in Korean history.

In 1989, Choi began writing full-time after moving to Cambridge, Massachusetts, to be close to her daughters, who both attended Harvard. The painstaking process of translating her memories into English produced a manuscript that was more than six hundred pages long. Choi had to trim the book, cutting much of the detail of her horrible experience. *Year of Impossible Goodbyes* was published in 1991.

Based on Choi's final months in Pyongyang in 1945, the book follows a girl named Sookan and her family as they endure the Japanese occupation of Korea. Cruel Captain Narita destroys everything of value and beauty, including Grandfather's beloved pine tree. But he cannot crush the family's spirit.

The faith of Sookan was inspired by the author's mother, whose optimism prevailed in the face of despair. "When our country was suffering, she made me feel that this was not the way things were all over the world," says Choi. "She always saw good in people."[9]

When the Soviet troops take over, Sookan and her brother, Inchun, realize their only hope is to risk a dangerous escape from their beloved homeland.

Year of Impossible Goodbyes received the Judy Lopez Award from the Women's National Book Association and was chosen as an American Library Association Notable Children's Book. The New York Public Library named it as one of the Best Books for the Teen Age in 1992.

The critically acclaimed book was embraced by young readers. Choi received so many letters that she decided to continue Sookan's story. The sequels, *Echoes of the White Giraffe* (1993) and *Gathering of Pearls* (1994), follow Sookan from a refugee school in Pusan, Korea, to college in the United States. "Ms. Choi writes of social, political and personal hurts in a context few young Americans today have experienced," commented one reviewer. "Yet she tells of more than dislocation, she tells of Sookan's personal growth, indeed her triumph."[10]

Readers of the Sookan trilogy often ask Ms. Choi about what happened to the real people in the story. Sadly, she learned that several had been killed by the Soviets. Since then, communication has been

Sook Nyul Choi's autobiographical book, *Year of Impossible Goodbyes*, has touched many young fans.

completely severed between North and South Korea. "When the moon is full and shining bright, I look up and imagine that those friends and relatives who did survive are staring up at the same moon," reflected Choi. "I keep praying that Korea will once again be united, and that everyone will live in peace and freedom."[11]

Her brother—Inchun in the book—is a medical doctor in Korea. He often visits Choi in the United States.

Sook Nyul Choi has expanded into picture books. Drawing on her experiences as a schoolteacher and as a mother, she has created *Halmoni and the Picnic* (1993), *Yummi and Halmoni's Trip* (1997), and *The Best Older Sister* (1997). In these stories, which also involve Korean characters, the author hopes to "help children understand their feelings better, and better understand the feelings of others."[12]

Through her writing, Sook Nyul Choi has come to terms with the vast scope of her life. "Pain, joy, dark, light . . . they're all part of the picture," she said. "You learn to forgive how bad the pain is or it is wasted on you."[13]

When Choi was little, her mother told her that every time you suffer, a thin gold leaf comes out of your heart, passes through your mouth, and goes up to heaven. "As a child," said Choi, "I used to imagine that when I died I would go up to heaven and see all those gold sparkles and go crunching through the gold leaves that came from my heart."[14]

Maxine Hong Kingston

Maxine Hong Kingston
(1940–   )

As a child, Maxine Hong Kingston struggled to speak. She was shy, and she was fearful about communicating in English for the first time. So she withdrew into complete silence when she entered school. "My silence was thickest—total—during the three years that I covered my school paintings with black paint. I painted layers of black over houses and flowers and suns. . . . I was making a stage curtain, and it was the moment before the curtain parted or rose."[1]

Despite her struggles, Maxine knew she had an outlet. "In a way, I've never been silent. . . . While I've had problems speaking, I've always been a writer."[2]

When Kingston's autobiographical story *The Woman Warrior* first appeared in 1976, it was embraced by readers and critics alike. A blend of myth, history, and autobiography, Kingston's writing was truly unique. For many readers it was their first real look at Chinese American life and culture. For her groundbreaking work, Kingston has been called the "godmother" of Asian American literature.[3]

Kingston's father left China in 1924 to seek a new life in the United States. When he arrived in New York City, he took the name Tom, after Thomas Edison. A teacher and scholar, Tom Hong could not find work in his profession, so he took a job in a laundry. He sent money back home to his wife, Ying Lan, who completed her medical training in China. In 1939, she left behind a successful medical practice to join Tom in New York.

After Tom Hong was cheated out of his share of a New York laundry business, they moved to Stockton, California, where Maxine (Ting Ting) was born on October 27, 1940.

Her father's new business, the New Port Laundry, became the center of family life for Maxine and her five younger siblings. Other Chinese people in Stockton would gather there to trade "talk-stories," personal versions of Chinese history, myths, and family tales. Maxine's mother, Brave Orchid in *The Woman Warrior*, was a master storyteller. "Night after night my mother would talk-story until we fell asleep," wrote Maxine. "I could not tell where the stories left off and the dreams began."[4]

The vivid tales of family ancestors and ancient legends would later form the basis for Kingston's books. But as a child, Maxine was haunted by the stories; by her silent father, who screamed in his sleep; and by her powerful mother, who was often cruel to Maxine. Together with her siblings, Maxine would escape to explore the creeks and hobo trails of Stockton.

Maxine spoke only Chinese in her early years. But by the age of nine, she was writing creatively in English. "I was in fourth grade and all of a sudden this poem started coming out of me," she said. "On and on I went, oblivious to everything. It is a bad habit that doesn't go away."[5]

Although she received little encouragement from her parents, Maxine excelled in school and earned straight A's. Eleven scholarships enabled her to attend the University of California at Berkeley. Growing up, Maxine had experienced conflict with her mother, so she was eager to leave. In *The Woman Warrior*, she lashes out at her mother: "Even if I am stupid and talk funny and get sick, I won't let you turn me into a slave or wife. I'm getting out of here. . . . And I don't want to listen to any more of your stories; they have no logic. They scramble me up."[6]

Her first year at Berkeley was difficult. She found herself alone for the first time, without her family. "I got terrible grades at first," she said. "Even my writing didn't save me."[7] She had majored in engineering as a practical career choice, but then switched to English literature.

In a Berkeley English class, Maxine met actor Earll Kingston. In 1962, after Maxine earned her bachelor's degree, the two married. Their son, Joseph Lawrence Chung Mei, was born in 1964. Knowing she would have to make a living to support her writing, Maxine returned to Berkeley, where she earned her teaching certificate.

The Kingstons joined the peace movement on campus and protested against the Vietnam War. "The values of the time matched mine so well," recalls Maxine. "We in Berkeley thought we were going to change the world."[8]

In 1965, the couple taught high school in Hayward, California. But as the antiwar movement became more violent, and their friends became heavily involved with drugs, the Kingstons sought a more peaceful environment.

In 1967, on their way to Japan, the Kingstons stopped in Hawaii—and stayed for seventeen years. Far from home, Maxine was able to gain the perspective she needed to write her autobiographical book *The Woman Warrior: Memoirs of a Girlhood Among Ghosts*, which was published in 1976.

Kingston's story of growing up in two cultures—Chinese and American—is interwoven with Chinese myth and the stories of her ancestors. Kingston tries

Maxine grew up torn between two cultures—American and Chinese—and both influence her writing.

to come to terms with it all, including the tragic life of "No-Name Aunt," who drowned herself in the family well. "My aunt haunts me—her ghost drawn to me because now, after fifty years of neglect, I alone devote pages of paper to her," wrote Kingston.[9]

In another chapter Kingston dreams of becoming a powerful woman warrior like the legendary Fa Mu Lan of her mother's talk-stories. "The swordswoman and I are not so dissimilar," she wrote. "What we have in common are the words at our back. . . . And I have so many words."[10]

Kingston relates Brave Orchid's story and the difficult relationship she and her daughter shared. Only after she finished the book did Kingston fully realize her mother's influence. "My mother is the creative one, with visions and the stories to tell. . . . She's the great inspiration."[11]

The Woman Warrior was a huge success, winning the National Book Critics Circle Award for nonfiction. At the awards ceremony, the four-foot-nine-inch Kingston could not see over the podium, so she bent around the side and delivered a moving acceptance speech.

The best-selling book touched many readers, particularly Chinese American women who recognized some of their own lives in the story. But her writing was never intended to represent all Chinese Americans, asserted Kingston. "Each artist has a unique voice," she said. She looks forward to the time when "many of us are published and then we will be able to see the range of viewpoints, of visions, of what it is to be Chinese American."[12]

In 1980 Kingston published *China Men.* A companion volume to *Woman Warrior, China Men* tells the male side of Kingston's family story. In the "Gold Mountain" land of America, Kingston's father and other Chinese Americans make their contribution to their new country, from building the first transcontinental railway to serving in the armed forces during the Vietnam War. By writing about the efforts of Chinese Americans and the discrimination they faced, Kingston said she was "claiming America." "We belong here," she explained. "This is our country, this is our history and we are a part of America."[13] Another best-seller, *China Men* was honored with the National Book Award for nonfiction and the American Book Award.

Along with her success, Kingston has also encountered criticism. Some critics say her version of Chinese myth is not accurate. By changing the stories, Kingston explains, she is continuing the talk-story tradition. "We have to do more than record myth," she said. "The way I keep the old Chinese myths alive is by telling them in a new American way."[14]

In 1984, Kingston made her first trip to China, a country she had "made up" in her books.[15] Seeing her family's village renewed her faith in her mother's talk-stories and her own imagination. "Many of the colors, and the smells, the people, the faces, the incidents, were much as I imagined."[16] That same year the Kingstons moved to Los Angeles, and then to Oakland in 1987. Their son, Joseph, a musician, remained in Hawaii.

Kingston published her first novel, *Tripmaster Monkey: His Fake Book,* in 1989. Partly inspired by her Berkeley days, the story follows Wittman Ah Sing, a fifth-generation Chinese American, and his adventures in San Francisco during the 1960s. While the reviews were mixed, one critic called *Tripmaster Monkey* "the great American novel of the sixties."[17]

In 1990, Kingston was thrilled to return to the University of California at Berkeley, this time as a distinguished professor of English. The following year, however, was marked by loss. One month after her father's death, Kingston's home was consumed in the Oakland Hills fire. Everything was destroyed, including her work in progress, "The Fourth Book of Peace." Seeing the ashes of her manuscript discouraged Kingston. Moving on, she called on others to contribute to her new book, tentatively titled "The Fifth Book of Peace."

In 1997 Kingston went to the White House, where President Bill Clinton awarded her the National Humanities Medal. The highest national honor given to an American artist, the award credited Kingston with creating a new literary form and illuminating the Chinese American experience. In the process, she has encouraged others to tell their own stories. Amy Tan and other Asian American writers have named Kingston as an inspiration. Still others—who are now reading her books in school— are yet to be heard.

For her, Kingston says, writing is as natural an activity as eating and breathing. Whether she was born that way, or whether it is because she was raised in a storytelling culture, she does not know. But she believes that all people have a need to express them- selves creatively. Of writing, she says, "I will be doing this thing forever."[18]

Marie G. Lee

Marie G. Lee

(1964–)

The popular cheerleading captain at her high school, Marie Lee was thrilled when she won a makeover sponsored by *Seventeen* magazine. "At last," recalled Marie, "*Seventeen* was going to turn me into one of those All American girls!"[1] But afterward, when she looked in the mirror, she was shocked to see that she had been given a "China chop" haircut, and her eyes were lined in an exotic Cleopatra look. Marie felt humiliated.

Growing up the only Asian American in her neighborhood, Marie said, "I thought of myself as culturally white, or at least, All American. Other people—even my friends—saw me as a China doll."[2] At that moment, Marie realized she was neither.

Her own experiences growing up have helped shape Marie's career as a writer of young adult novels. "I write coming of age stories of people, who, for some reason, feel different from those around them," says Lee.[3]

Marie's father, William Lee, worked as a U.S. Army translator during the Korean War, while also attending medical school. Searching for better opportunities, he and his wife, Grace Lee, left Korea in 1953 and settled in California. Eventually William secured a job in Minnesota as an anesthesiologist. The Lees settled in the small town of Hibbing, and soon after started a family. Marie G. Lee was born April 25, 1964, the third of four children.

In Hibbing—also the hometown of the famous folk singer Bob Dylan—the Lees lived a comfortable, middle-class life. They were the only Asian family in the region, which was predominantly Scandinavian. As Marie has said, "Everyone is blond. It was hard to fit in."[4] Wanting their children to grow up as American as possible, Marie's parents never spoke Korean at home.

While her parents encouraged academic achievement, they also allowed Marie a lot of privacy, and she spent a lot of time "just dreaming." It was this time alone, says Lee, that led her to become a writer.[5]

Because she was shy and bookish as a child, Marie withdrew to the library, which also offered refuge from some unpleasant encounters at school. "I didn't have anything like [the books I now write] when I was growing up and wish I did," said Lee. "I really wish there was a book describing how it felt to be called a 'chink,' to have teachers making nasty jokes about how Koreans eat dog."[6] Instead, Lee turned to books dealing with alienation, such as *The Catcher in the Rye* and *The Outsiders.*

From the age of three or four, Marie remembers hearing the word "chink" and experiencing other racial taunts. But she views her high-school years as a wonderful period in her life. "It was a time when I first felt really intense about things," said Marie. "I could look at the sunset and feel profound about it."[7]

Although it was "not cool to be smart at my school," said Marie, she excelled academically, which pleased her parents.[8] At the time, Marie wondered why she had to do extra book reports while her friends played. "I know my parents felt that because we were kids of color, it might be harder for us to succeed," said Lee later, "and that education is a big leveling tool."[9] Today, she realizes that if she had followed the path of most of her friends, she might never have gone on to college.

Her father hoped Marie and her siblings would become physicians like himself. But early on, Marie was drawn to writing—"ever since I got my first type-writer, and I saw how cool the words looked when they were typed," she said. "My first book was made out of scratch paper and was held together by yarn."[10]

When she was just sixteen, Marie sold her first

Marie's parents wanted her to fit in, and as a little girl she considered herself an all-American kid.

article to *Seventeen.* That first sale made writing seem easy, but for the next ten years Marie's work was rejected by publishers.

In 1982, Lee entered Smith College, in Northampton, Massachusetts, where she tried different fields. But she dropped out of pre-med after the first course—she was simply too squeamish for medicine. Transferring to Brown University, in Providence, Rhode Island, Lee graduated in 1986. She earned a degree in economics so she could get a "real" job, she said, "but in my heart of hearts, I knew I was going to be a writer."[11]

After graduation, Lee moved to New York City. Her first job out of college was with a research firm that used computer-generated models to forecast the economy. It paid well, Lee said, but "for an aspiring writer, this wasn't a great job." Lee then worked on Wall Street for Goldman Sachs, an investment bank. In every spare moment, she worked on her writing. "I was getting up at 4:30 in the morning," remembered Lee, "writing for two hours, going to work, then falling asleep at work."[12]

Despite her exhaustion, and a bout with mononucleosis, a viral infection that causes extreme fatigue, Lee finished the manuscript of her first book in 1989. It made the rounds of the publishers—and was rejected fifteen times. During this period, Lee began a correspondence with author Judy Blume, who encouraged Lee, urging her not to give up. Lee's agent agreed to take the manuscript to one last place.

Houghton Mifflin bought *Finding My Voice*, which was published in 1992.

The story centers on Ellen Sung, like Lee the only Asian in her Minnesota high school. With her sister attending Harvard, Ellen feels pressured by her parents to succeed. At school she is forced to cope with other issues. Ellen's growing romance with a popular boy, Topper, forces a confrontation between Ellen and a bigoted classmate. But Ellen faces up to the challenge and emerges with a new self-confidence. For its depth and candor, *Finding My Voice* was widely praised and won several awards. One critic said, "The story allows readers first to flinch in recognition and then to look into their own hearts."[13]

"I think first novels tend to look directly back into the author's life," commented Lee.[14] Though Ellen's story wasn't exactly hers, Lee did share similar experiences, including those involving bigotry. "Looking back, I see that there was a real potential for me as an impressionable adolescent to lose my self-esteem," said Lee, "and if I hadn't had the support of my parents and friends, perhaps I would've just become a bitter, hateful person instead of having the experience make me learn to stand up for myself."[15]

In 1993, Houghton Mifflin released Marie G. Lee's second novel, *If It Hadn't Been for Yoon Jun*. This story, geared for younger readers, concerns Alice, also a Korean American character. But this time, Lee wanted to explore the perspective of growing up in a white family. Adopted by the Larsens, Alice has no interest in her Korean heritage. When a Korean boy, Yoon Jun Lee, enters her junior high school, Alice snobbishly rejects him. Forced to work with him on a school project, Alice forms a friendship with Yoon Jun and gains an understanding of Korean culture.

The following year saw the release of *Saying Goodbye*. In her third novel Lee continues the story of Ellen Sung as she embarks on her college career. Since then, Lee has branched out with other books. *Necessary Roughness* (1996) was written from the perspective of a male character, set against a backdrop of high school football.

After her 1997 marriage to Karl Jacoby, a history professor, Lee published her next book. "A multicultural R. L. Stine-ish" mystery is how Lee describes *Night of the Chupacabras* (1998), a spooky adventure tale set in rural Mexico, where her husband spent part of his childhood.[16]

For her next project, Lee journeyed to Korea. Awarded a Fulbright scholarship in 1998, she traveled the country collecting oral histories of birth mothers who gave up children for adoption in the United States. Learning the language was a challenge for Lee. She also had to earn the trust of her interview subjects. Lee hoped to create a book that would give voice to these women, revealing the hardships they faced and fostering greater understanding of the adoption experience.

In addition to her books, Lee writes for literary anthologies and other journals. She has also lectured and taught creative writing at Yale University in New Haven, Connecticut. Despite her hectic personal schedule, Lee remains active in Asian American organizations, including the Asian American Writer's Workshop, which she cofounded in 1992.

When asked when she will be through writing about the "race thing," Marie Lee answered, "Probably never." In order to write with honesty, Lee believes, a writer must know herself first. "And for me," wrote Lee, "being an American of Korean descent and being a writer are inextricably linked."[17]

In writing books that deal honestly with prejudice and other challenges of growing up, Marie G. Lee discovered her own unique voice, one that is still evolving.

Bette Bao Lord
(1938–   )

"Only yesterday," remembered Bette Bao Lord, "resting my chin on the rails of the S.S. *Marylinx*, I peered into the mist for Mei Guo, beautiful country. It refused to appear. Then, within a blink, there was the golden gate, more like the portals to heaven than the arches of a man-made bridge."[1]

Today a best-selling author and respected activist for human rights, Lord recalls the single most important event in her life: her emigration from China to America. "Everyone wonders about the roads not taken," she wrote, "only we immigrants can point to the fork that above all else has shaped our destinies."[2]

On November 3, 1938, Bette was born in Shanghai, China, to Dora and Sandys Bao. Studying

Bette Bao Lord

the lines in her tiny palm, her grandfather declared, "Her life will be full, her spirit strong. This baby will have a rich passage."[3]

Following World War II, Sandys Bao, an electrical engineer, went to the United States on business for the Chinese government. In 1946, he sent for his wife and two of his daughters, including eight-year-old Bette. Still an infant, Bette's younger sister Sansan was left behind with relatives.

The day after arriving in Brooklyn, New York, Bette was enrolled in the fifth grade. "So I was the shortest student by a head or two in class," recalls Lord.[4]

Communist rebels won control of China in 1949, and the Baos knew they could not return home. Sandys Bao had been a colonel in the Nationalist army and surely would have been arrested. It would also be too dangerous to try to get Sansan, who remained in China.

The Baos settled in Teaneck, New Jersey, where Bette grew up. Popular among her classmates, Bette was also an excellent student. In 1954 she won a scholarship to Tufts University near Boston, Massachusetts.

She started out as a chemistry major because "every Chinese child is supposed to grow up to be an '-ist,' as in scientist," said Lord. (Lord pointed out that in middle age she had become an *-ist*—as in novelist.)[5] After accumulating a large "breakage bill" in the lab, Bette learned she was in danger of flunking.

So she decided to switch her major to history and political science, earning her bachelor's degree in 1959 and a master's degree the following year. In graduate school, Bette met Winston Lord, but she decided to hold off on marriage. "I was proud and did not want to marry him without having made my mark," said Bette.[6]

After serving as an administrator at the University of Hawaii, Bette headed for a job in Washington, D.C., where Winston was working in the U.S. Foreign Service. Despite a warning that marriage to an immigrant would hurt his career, Winston married Bette in 1963.

Meanwhile, the Chinese government had allowed Sansan Bao to "visit her ailing mother" in Hong Kong. This was actually a scheme that enabled the Baos to help Sansan escape to America. Separated for more than fifteen years, Sansan and her family were reunited in 1962.

Hearing about Sansan's incredible story, friends thought it would make a great book. "I stumbled into writing," said Lord. "I wrote . . . my sister's story because she only spoke Chinese and I knew of no writers who did. Ignorant of how difficult it was to get into print, I took up the task."[7] Lord quit her job and finished writing the book in only nine months.

By chance, Lord met a publisher who agreed to listen to her story—briefly. "Only five minutes!" Lord panicked. "So I talked and talked as fast as I could until I had my sister's story out."[8]

The publisher liked what he heard, and in 1964 Harper & Row released *Eighth Moon: The True Story of a Young Girl's Life in Communist China*. It was a hit with readers and critics. One review said the book revealed much about Communist China "through the little human details of how Sansan lived, worked, and thought."[9] Just twenty-six years old, Lord did not believe she had earned her success. "I was scared to raise a pen for the next ten years," she remembered.[10]

During this time, the Lords became a family. In 1964, they welcomed a daughter, Lisa (Elizabeth Pillsbury). Their son, Winston Bao, called Win, was born four years later. For a time, Bette turned away from writing.

The Lords spent the years 1965 to 1967 in Geneva, Switzerland, where Winston had been sent as part of a U.S. diplomatic team. There Bette taught and performed modern dance, which she had studied since college. After they returned home, Winston joined President Richard Nixon's administration as a top aide to Secretary of State Henry Kissinger.

In 1973, Bette traveled to China and reunited with the family she had not seen since childhood. When she got off the train in Shanghai, she ran to embrace them. "And that of course was very un-Chinese," remembered Lord, "but I think they forgave this stranger who had come home."[11] She planned a journal about their experiences. But fearing her family might be punished by the oppressive

Communist government, she decided to write a novel instead.

In the small town of Nederland, Colorado, where the Lord family moved in 1974, Bette began writing. Aided by cigars and coffee, she worked from midnight to 5:00 A.M., when her kids were asleep. Writing her first novel was a difficult, six-year process, during which Lord wrote and rewrote some chapters as many as twenty times.

Published in 1981, *Spring Moon: A Novel of China* is the sweeping tale of the Chang family through five generations. Nominated for a National Book Award, *Spring Moon* is often regarded as Lord's finest book.

Lord next turned to her own life story for *In the Year of the Boar and Jackie Robinson* (1984), her first book for children. Based on her early years in America, Lord depicts the humorous adventures of a ten-year-old Chinese girl, Shirley Temple Wong, as she adjusts to life in her new country. At first Shirley has trouble making friends. Then she discovers baseball. This uplifting story continues to be a favorite among schoolchildren.

In 1985, the Lords moved to China when Winston was named U.S. ambassador to that country. Because of her Chinese heritage and ability to speak the language, Bette was a great help to her husband. She was often called an "unofficial ambassador." Her duties, however, prevented her from working on her fourth novel.

Instead, Lord devoted herself to cultural activities, turning the U.S. Embassy in Beijing into a meeting place for artists and intellectuals. They gathered there to view American films and to dance and talk freely. She helped distribute American books in China, and with royalty payments from her writing she staged Broadway performances for the Chinese public. Despite her efforts, China's Communist government continued to restrict artistic expression. "It pains me to think of the untapped talent . . . ," said Lord, "the books that haven't been written, the paintings that haven't been painted."[12] However, Lord remained hopeful that the Chinese people would one day gain more artistic freedom.

In the spring of 1989, student-led pro-democracy demonstrations arose throughout China, including in Beijing. While Winston returned to Washington, Bette stayed behind to report for CBS News and *Newsweek* magazine.

Standing in Beijing's Tiananmen Square one May night, Lord marveled at the hope and excitement that had spread across China. However, just days after her return to the United States, hope turned to tragedy in Tiananmen Square. On June 6, China's army opened fire on the unarmed student demonstrators. An estimated five thousand people were killed, and hundreds more were imprisoned or executed.

The tragic event inspired Lord to write *Legacies: A Chinese Mosaic*, published in 1990. "When

Lord has used her position to speak out for human rights around the world.

Americans saw the people in Tiananmen Square last year," she said, "they just saw a sea of black-haired people. I felt that I had to write *Legacies* because I wanted to put faces and stories with what happened there."[13]

During Lord's stay in China, people from all walks of life met with her, telling their stories into her tape recorder. Selected from six hundred tapes, the stories in *Legacies* include the experience of Lord's beloved aunt Goo Ma. Because she was a teacher, Goo Ma suffered beatings and imprisonment at the hands of the Communists. Held for six months in a windowless broom closet in her school, Goo Ma vowed to live to see the day when she would be a teacher once more. Incredibly, she did.

Legacies was named one of the best nonfiction books of 1990 by *Time* magazine.

Lord's next book, *The Middle Heart*, was published in 1996. The novel traces the lives of three devoted friends who endure the dramatic events of twentieth-century China. *The Middle Heart*, wrote one book critic, "is in keeping with Lord's humane vision of a courageous people who are victims of history."[14]

In recent years, Lord has become active in the human rights movement, joining Freedom House, an organization that works toward preserving political and civil rights around the world. In 1994, Lord became its chairwoman.

She continues to speak out for freedom and equality. As her native China faces an uncertain future, Lord remains hopeful. "I believe in the Chinese people," she states, their brave stand in Tiananmen Square still fresh in her memory.[15]

Bette Bao Lord remembers, too, her immigrant roots. They give her a special appreciation of the freedom enjoyed in America and the good fortune that brought her to its shores.

Kyoko Mori

(1957–   )

"My mother's suicide singled me out as a girl without a mother," wrote Kyoko Mori. "No matter how much my friends loved me, they could never understand what I was going through. I felt sealed inside by unhappiness, unable to talk about it or ask for help."[1]

Drawing upon her own life experience to write her first novel, *Shizuko's Daughter*, Kyoko Mori transforms into words the unspoken emotion of a childhood devastated by loss.

Kyoko Mori was born March 9, 1957, in Kobe, Japan. Together with her father, Hiroshi, an engineer; her mother, Takako; and her younger brother, Jumpei, Kyoko lived in the comfortable suburbs of

Kyoko Mori

Kobe, a beautiful city nestled between the mountains and the sea.

"There was a story in my family that I learned to talk before I walked," says Mori, who was born with both hips dislocated.[2] She spent her first eighteen months in leg harnesses to correct the problem.

Unlike her cold and indifferent father, Kyoko's mother, Takako, was a gentle, perceptive soul who nurtured the children with creativity. "My mother had never been content just to live and be comfortable," wrote Mori. "She always wanted something more—some form of beauty."[3]

Takako filled their apartment with embroidery, planted a small garden of colorful flowers, and took Kyoko to art exhibits. She also surrounded the children with books and writings. When she was very young, Mori remembered, her mother bought her a blank notebook. "After I learned enough symbols and characters in school, I would write down the stories and she would draw the pictures. They were mostly adventure stories, about girls going to faraway, magical places with their cats or dolls and coming back victorious and rich."[4]

Another major influence was her maternal grandfather, a former teacher. Writing in his journal every day, he first exposed Kyoko to the discipline of writing.

"These two people in my family gave me the idea that writing was something we did every day or even every week with enjoyment," recalled Mori.[5]

Little Kyoko Mori at her grandparents' house. As an author, Mori writes about two lives—her childhood in Japan and her adult years in America.

But pleasurable pursuits and the love of her children could not overcome Takako's profound sadness. At the heart of her troubles was her unhappy marriage to the stern Hiroshi.

One day in March 1969, twelve-year-old Kyoko and her younger brother came home and found their mother lying motionless on the floor. She had committed suicide, using gas.

Their father left the traumatized children alone with the body. After sending Jumpei upstairs, Kyoko covered her mother with a blanket and waited. Incredibly, Hiroshi made Kyoko go to the police station to make the report.

The night after her mother's death, the house still permeated with gas fumes, Kyoko went to her mother's room. "I pulled out the red notebook. . . . I had known about the journal during her life, though I never would have touched it then. I wanted to be the first, perhaps the only person to read her words."[6]

Only a few weeks later, her father's mistress, Michiko, moved in. She became Kyoko's stepmother a year later. "Your mother is gone, and you have a new mother," her father declared. "It's time for some changes."[7]

A petty and jealous woman, Michiko would often pack her bags and threaten to leave. Blaming Kyoko, her father beat the girl repeatedly. "'Don't look at me with that impertinent face,' he would say as his hand flew toward my cheek. It didn't matter whether I was frowning, smiling, or trying to keep my face absolutely blank. My face was always an impertinent face."[8]

The abuse continued into her teens, and Kyoko planned an escape route over neighboring rooftops. "Every night, I slept in my clothes and tennis shoes, with a big chair pushed against my door, ready in case he came in the middle of the night to kill me with my stepmother's butcher knife, something he had threatened several times to do."[9]

One of the last decisions Kyoko had made with her mother was to attend Kobe Jogakuin, a private school. A progressive school founded by Americans in the 1870s, Kobe Jogakuin emphasized the arts and languages. It also allowed students plenty of freedom, unlike the rigid atmosphere more common to Japanese schools.

Schoolwork provided some respite from home, but Kyoko was forever shadowed by her devastating loss.

As a junior in high school, Kyoko traveled to Mesa, Arizona, as an exchange student. "It was a revelation for me. For the first time in my life I was away from the social constrictions of my society. In Arizona, I felt real freedom," she said.[10]

Returning to Japan, Mori finished high school and two years of college, during which she concentrated on writing. In 1977, she realized her dream of returning to the United States. She won a scholarship to Rockford College, near Chicago. There Mori majored in English and creative writing, earning a bachelor's degree in 1979.

Mori and her writing flourished with the help of her teachers "and from being in a community of people who were serious about becoming writers," she said.[11] A master's degree followed in 1981 from the University of Wisconsin, Milwaukee, where she also received a Ph.D. in English and creative writing in 1984.

It was in graduate school that she began writing about her experiences growing up in Japan. In a story about an old woman, Mori said, "I wanted to find out, through writing, what it might be like to be my grandmother. . . ."[12] That story later formed the basis of her first novel.

Mori became a naturalized U.S. citizen in 1984 and married Charles Brock, an elementary-school teacher. The following year she accepted an associate professorship of English at Saint Norbert College in De Pere, Wisconsin.

On a 1990 sabbatical from teaching, Mori visited Japan for the first time in thirteen years. Returning to what she called the "landscape of my childhood," Mori reexamined painful memories and endured an awkward reunion with her father.[13]

Meanwhile, Mori's stories were circulating among publishers. At Henry Holt, an editor wanted to adapt them into a young adult book. Mori rearranged the autobiographical material and fleshed out the story. "This rewriting forced me to be more honest with myself," she said.[14]

Shizuko's Daughter was published in 1993, the same year her father died. It is the moving coming-of-age story of a young girl, Yuki, who must cope with her mother's suicide. Mori's first novel was called a "jewel of a book. One of those rarities that shine out only a few times in a generation." *Shizuko's Daughter* won citations from the American Library Association, *The New York Times*, and many young fans.[15]

Mori's writing is praised for its unique subtlety. She explains: "What I like to do in writing is to get to the edge of saying it all and then hold back. I like to let the images speak and to be understated."[16] She also writes without a particular audience in mind. "Mostly, I write the stories and poems I want to tell and hear," she told an interviewer.[17]

In 1994, Mori published *Fallout*, a collection of poems. A year later it was followed by a novel, *One Bird*. In Mori's second novel for young adults, Megumi, a teenage girl, is deeply affected by her parents' separation and becomes increasingly isolated. One day she discovers a wounded bird, which leads to a job with a veterinarian. As Megumi cares for wounded birds to be released back into the wild, she renews her own life.

Mori chose to write in the first person in *The Dream of Water: A Memoir* (1995). Recounting her 1990 return to Japan, the book details Mori's life following the loss of her mother, and the torment she endured at the hands of her father and stepmother. There is a joyous reunion with relatives on both sides. Particularly touching are moments spent with her mother's family, contact with whom had been severed by her father.

Inevitably, Mori faces her father and stepmother in a painful and strange meeting. Ever spiteful, Michiko criticizes the way Kyoko's mother's raised her. Kyoko's father, who has not seen his daughter in thirteen years, abruptly leaves to take a nap. Despite these difficult events, Mori gains some perspective on her own feelings, as well as a greater understanding of her mother's life.

Since then, Mori has divorced and relocated to Cambridge, Massachusetts, where she continues her teaching career at Harvard University. Her 1998 book of essays, *Polite Lies*, explores the different ways in which Japanese and Americans communicate and how she herself is a blend of both cultures.

Although she does not regret leaving Japan, Mori carries on her mother's legacy. "All these years later," wrote Mori, "my conviction remains the same: I speak her words though I speak them in another language."[18]

Bharati Mukherjee

Bharati Mukherjee
(1940–   )

"I had been so sheltered," said Bharati Mukherjee of her early life.[1] Born into a well-to-do Hindu family of Brahmin caste—the top of India's social order—Mukherjee could never walk alone on the street. She never touched money; a servant was always by her side to pay for purchases. She never learned to swim or drive a car.

Along with all women of her social standing, Mukherjee was trained to lower her head in the presence of men. To voice her opinion or think independently was forbidden.

Like many of the heroines in her books, Bharati Mukherjee wanted more than the narrow life that fate had granted her.

Bharati Mukherjee was born July 27, 1940, in Calcutta, India, to Sudhir Lal, who owned a pharmaceutical business, and his wife, Bina Mukherjee.

Along with her parents and two sisters, Bharati lived among more than thirty relatives, as well as servants. "Having been a lonely bookish child, she remembered, "[I] was always looking for a quiet private corner of a crowded room in which I could read my books and be on my own."[2]

While she felt a lack of privacy at home, Bharati was isolated from the outside world. She was largely confined to her family's private compound, surrounded by bodyguards. Mukherjee later recalled, "Even in my privileged part of Calcutta, I was doomed to a very restrictive life."[3]

The only time Bharati saw her mother was at mealtime. "As she fed me, she would tell me stories. Whether they were Hindu epics of historical figures roaming the earth, she made the characters come alive. It was from her that I learned the love of a good story."[4]

At the age of eight, her life changed dramatically. Her father's business took the family to Europe, where her mother enrolled her daughters in British and Swiss schools.

For her efforts, however, Bina Mukherjee suffered verbal and physical abuse by her in-laws. Bharati recalls the harsh words of her grandmother: "Who do you think you are? Wasting money and effort for daughters?"[5] Crediting her mother for her education,

Mukherjee once said: "It was because of her that I am the person that I am today."[6]

Upon their return to Calcutta, Bina Mukherjee asserted herself once again. She insisted that the family live in a house of their own. They moved to a fashionable area, where Bharati and her sisters attended an elite school for girls.

An avid reader since age three, Bharati read many classic books in both Bengali, her native language, and English. At the age of nine, she began her own novel. The story was about a child detective.

After secondary school, Bharati entered the University of Calcutta, where she earned a bachelor's degree in 1959. While she was in graduate school, her father brought about the next phase of her life. One evening he asked a dinner guest: "I want this daughter to be a writer; where shall I send her?"[7] With that, Mukherjee was on her way to America.

In 1961, she arrived at the University of Iowa on a scholarship to attend a writers' workshop. "Suddenly I didn't have to answer to anyone. I . . . wore pants and could stay up . . . and drink coffee until 9 P.M. I blossomed."[8]

Thrilled with her newfound freedom, Mukherjee nevertheless lacked experience living on her own. In those days she wore only saris—traditional Indian dresses—and sandals, even in the midwestern snow. Years later, she could still recall her chilled toes. Offered a pair of boots by the director of the writing program, she went to his home to get them. It was there that she met follow student Clark Blaise.

After a two-week courtship, the young writers were married above the campus coffee shop during a lunch break. It was 1963, the same year she earned a master of fine arts degree in creative writing. Mukherjee waited until after the wedding to tell her parents, who were in the midst of arranging her marriage to a scientist back in India.

Mukherjee gave up her privileged class when she married Blaise, but her parents came to accept him after the birth of their children. In 1964, Bart Anand was born, and three years later, they had a second son, Bernard Sudhir.

Blaise and Mukherjee struggled financially, taking on several teaching jobs while they pursued their writing. "I was brought up spectacularly rich—in the Third World sense—and have been spectacularly poor almost all my adult life," said Mukherjee. "At one time, I had to calculate whether I had enough money to buy orange juice as well as milk for breakfast."[9] Even years later, after the critical success of her books, Mukherjee would continue teaching to support herself.

In 1966, the family moved to Blaise's native Canada, where both taught at McGill University, in Montreal. Mukherjee earned a Ph.D. from the University of Iowa in 1969.

During this period she became a published writer with *The Tiger's Daughter* (1972). In what one reviewer called an "elegant first novel," an Indian-born woman marries an American, then returns home to discover an India different from the one she had known as a child.[10] Like her character, Mukherjee said that when she was writing the book she was "like a bridge, poised between two worlds."[11]

After a second novel, *Wife* (1975), Mukherjee wrote no fiction for a time. In February 1975, a kitchen fire raged through Mukherjee's home, destroying two thousand books, Indian tapestries, and original manuscripts. Devastated, Blaise and Mukherjee took their sons to India. The couple described their yearlong adventure in daily journals, which were published as a book, *Days and Nights in Calcutta* (1977).

In 1978, the family moved to Toronto, Canada. There Mukherjee encountered brutal racism. During a time when thousands of Asian refugees entered Canada, Mukherjee was spit on and physically assaulted. "I found myself constantly fighting battles against racial prejudice," said Mukherjee, who published articles and stories about the problem.[12] Although she values those years for strengthening her as a person and a writer, she knew she had to leave.[13]

In 1980, the family moved to Saratoga Springs, New York, where Mukherjee became an English professor at Skidmore College. She never regretted her decision. "Canada and the U.S. have very different ways of treating newcomers," commented Mukherjee.

"Here diversity is accepted; the melting pot helps the newcomer to feel more welcome."[14]

After the 1985 publication of *Darkness,* her first collection of stories, Mukherjee left Skidmore and moved around the country, following a series of teaching jobs in Atlanta, New Jersey, and New York City. Meanwhile, Blaise and their sons settled in Iowa City. Mukherjee looks forward to a time when they can live and work in the same city. In the meantime, they rely on frequent-flyer miles and fax machines to maintain their long-distance marriage.

In *The Middleman and Other Stories* (1988) Mukherjee had gained enough confidence to create stories about immigrants other than South Asians. From a Filipino woman in Atlanta to an Iraqi Jew in Queens, her characters make their way in America in stories brimming with passion, violence, and humor.

The Middleman sold only a few thousand copies, so it was a big surprise when it won the National Book Critics Circle Award for fiction. The award changed Mukherjee's life. Overnight, she became a literary celebrity.

With much anticipation, Mukherjee published her novel *Jasmine* in 1989. The personal transformation of an Indian woman who journeys to America was very well received. That same year *Glamour* magazine named Mukherjee as one of the eight women "who'll leave their mark on the 90's."

In 1990, Mukherjee headed west for a professorship at the University of California at Berkeley. There

Award-winning writer Bharati Mukherjee maintains a busy schedule of writing, teaching and lecturing.

she wrote what she calls "my most autobiographical novel."[15] The idea for this book began years earlier, when, at an exhibit, Mukherjee saw a painting that fascinated her. It pictured a blond, Anglo woman at the Mughal emperor's court in full Indian dress. "It leapt out at me," she said. "Who was she? What got her there? How did she survive?"[16]

The author spent eleven years researching historical details—from herbal cures to how pioneer surgeons repaired scalped heads—for a story inspired by that painting. A cross-cultural adventure tale set in both modern New England and seventeenth-century India, *The Holder of the World* (1993) was called "a work of crystalline perfection."[17]

Her seventh work of fiction, *Leave It to Me* (1997), takes place closer to home, in present-day San Francisco. Mukherjee keeps an apartment there, where she does most of her writing.

Where do her stories come from? Mukherjee can catch a haunting face in a crowd or bits of a conversation overheard on the subway, and from there she creates a whole story. "Then there are all these characters in my head," said the author. "They are all screaming their stories at me and whoever screams the loudest gets his story told."[18]

With her writing, Bharati Mukherjee shows how America has transformed her. At the same time, she has opened our eyes to other "new Americans," who criss-cross time, culture, and racial identity in her brilliant stories.

Amy Tan

(1952–   )

When she was a child, Amy Tan slept with a clothespin on her nose, hoping to change its Asian shape. She also thought it might make her more American if she ate less Chinese food.

By rejecting anything Chinese, Amy clashed with her mother. With her broken English, traditional dress, and other Chinese customs—such as serving fish with the heads still on—everything about Daisy Tan embarrassed young Amy. Mother and daughter shared a difficult relationship. During one of their many arguments, Daisy told her daughter, "You don't know little percent of me."[1]

Years later, when Amy Tan came to better understand Daisy, she dedicated her first book to her

Amy Tan

mother. An emotional story about mothers and daughters, *The Joy Luck Club* spoke to millions of readers, and became a much-loved best-seller.

Amy Tan was born in Oakland, California, on February 19, 1952. Her father, John Tan, had emigrated from China to the United States in 1947. He became both an engineer and a Baptist minister. Amy's mother, Daisy, the daughter of an upper-class Chinese family, arrived from Shanghai in 1942. In the United States, she met and married John Tan, and they had three children.

Like many immigrant parents, the Tans had high hopes for their children. "From the age of six," remembered Amy, "I was led to believe that I would grow up to be a neurosurgeon by trade and a concert pianist by hobby."[2]

Amy grew up thinking she could never please her parents. If she came home with a B they asked why it was not an A. Later, as an adult, Amy understood that her parents wanted only the best for her. But in her childhood, she felt enormous pressure, particularly from her mother.

When Amy was fourteen, the Tan family was struck by tragedy. Amy's sixteen-year-old brother, Peter, died suddenly of a brain tumor. Just seven months later their father also died of brain cancer.

It was then that their mother made a shocking announcement. Back in China, she had left three daughters from a previous marriage. She had planned to bring them to the United States, but Chinese law forced her to give up custody to the children's father, who had abused Daisy. After the Communists took over China in 1949, she had lost contact with the children.

Still grieving for her father and brother, Amy was devastated by the news. Who were these other daughters? she wondered. Amy began to view herself as the "bad" daughter and directed her anger at her mother. "We got into terrible battles by the time I reached my teens," remembered Tan. "It wasn't until my twenties that we began to get along."[3]

Believing their California home was cursed, Daisy took fifteen-year-old Amy and her younger brother, John Jr., to live in Europe. They eventually settled in Montreux, Switzerland, where Amy attended high school. She fell in with the drug crowd and was arrested when she was sixteen. Despite her teenage rebellion, Amy managed to graduate from high school.

After a year the Tans returned to the United States. In 1969, Amy enrolled at Linfield College in Oregon as a pre-med student. But Amy decided that medical school was not for her and switched her major to English. Her mother was so disappointed that she did not speak to Amy for six months.

In Oregon, Amy fell in love with Lou DeMattei. She followed Lou to California and eventually joined him at San Jose State University. There she earned her bachelor's degree in English and linguistics in 1973. A master's degree followed in 1974, the same year she married Lou, who became a tax attorney. As she began a doctoral fellowship in linguistics at the University of California at Berkeley, tragedy struck again.

During a robbery, one of Tan and her husband's close friends was brutally murdered. "For me, something broke inside," says Tan.[4] That same day she turned twenty-four. Tan took a hard look at what she was doing with her life.

Tan dropped out of the doctoral program and began working with disabled children. Of the jobs she held, working in special education was especially meaningful. "That experience was a crash course about humanity, what hope means and things that matter most," said Tan. "It was rewarding and sad and it helped me identify with many different kinds of people."[5] But the work was draining, and she left the field.

By 1983, Tan was working as a business writer, crafting speeches and reports for big corporations, including IBM and AT&T. Tan was earning a good living. At last her mother considered her a success. But working ninety hours a week took its toll. Exhausted and unhappy, Tan sought help from psychological counseling. But when her therapist kept falling asleep, Tan turned to other outlets: jazz piano lessons and writing stories.

The year 1986 marked another fateful event: Daisy Tan was rushed to the hospital. It was a turning point for both mother and daughter. Believing she was near death, Daisy wondered about her legacy, what Amy would remember. "I decided that if my mother was okay," said Amy, "I'd get to know her. I'd take her to China and I'd write a book."[6] Daisy recovered, and Amy, who had been encouraged by an agent, began an outline for a book.

The following year, Tan, her husband, and her mother went to China. Meeting her long-lost sisters for the first time, Tan said, "There was an instant bond."[7] The trip also helped Tan take pride in her Chinese heritage. She was finally able to say, "I'm both Chinese and American."[8]

When she came home, Tan learned that G. P. Putnam had bought her outline. In 1989, the publisher released *The Joy Luck Club*. Tan's dedication to her mother reads: "You asked me once what I would remember. This, and much more."[9]

In the book, four older Chinese women form the Joy Luck Club. For forty years they have gathered together for mahjong—a Chinese game—and for friendship and gossip. The book reveals the women's painful past and their troubled relationships with their Americanized daughters. "These moving and powerful stories share the irony, pain and sorrow of the imperfect ways in which mothers and daughters love each other," wrote one critic. "Tan's vision is courageous and insightful."[10] A teen reader reported being inspired "to be kinder to my own mother and to share in her memories of the past."[11] A runaway best-seller, *The Joy Luck Club* was nominated for the National Book Award.

The book was made into a feature film in 1994. Directed by Chinese American director Wayne Wang, with a screenplay cowritten by Tan, the movie was a surprise hit.

While Tan was working on the *Joy Luck* script, her publisher anxiously awaited her second book. There was incredible pressure on Tan to create another best-seller. Several projects were abandoned before she decided on a subject close to home.

To tell her mother's story, Tan videotaped Daisy as she talked about losing her own mother to suicide, her abusive first husband, and life in wartime China. Watching her mother recount her past, Amy realized Daisy's gift for storytelling. *The Kitchen God's Wife* was released in 1991 and quickly climbed the bestseller charts.

Tan's next book was her first for children. Illustrated by her good friend Gretchen Shields, *The Moon Lady* is a Chinese tale based on a chapter in *The Joy Luck Club*. Tan's second picture book appeared in 1994. Inspired by her own seventeen-year-old cat, *The Chinese Siamese Cat* tells the story of a naughty kitten, Sagwa, and how the Siamese cat got its unique markings.

Tan returned to writing novels in 1995 with *The Hundred Secret Senses*. The story describes the conflict between Olivia and her Chinese half-sister Kwan, who communicates with "yin people," or ghosts.

A trip to China helped Amy Tan take pride in her heritage and share her mother's memories. Tan's best-selling story about mothers and daughters, *The Joy Luck Club*, was the result.

The book was another success for Tan, although the supernatural aspect bothered some critics.

Like many popular writers, Tan has received her share of criticism. Many unfairly assume that her books are meant to represent Chinese Americans, or all Asians. She says her stories are not especially symbolic or about ethnic themes.

Tan must also cope with the many duties that come from being a best-selling author. Her hectic schedule includes book signings, lectures, and travel around the world. When Tan does sit down to write, she turns off the phone and works the entire day, sometimes forgetting to stop for a meal.

In her spare time Tan has been known to shoot a mean game of pool. She also plays the piano and, with husband Lou, enjoys skiing. A member of a band called the Rock Bottom Remainders, Tan sometimes sings rock and roll with other writers—including Dave Barry, Stephen King, and Barbara Kingsolver—to help raise money for literacy programs.

Reading is perhaps Tan's favorite hobby. She particularly enjoys writers of different cultures and first-person stories. "I write for the reasons I read," she explained. "I read to startle my mind, to tingle my spine, to take the blinders off. Fiction is my confidant and companion for life."[12]

Yoshiko Uchida

Yoshiko Uchida

(1921–1992)

On December 7, 1941, Yoshiko Uchida and her family were sitting down to Sunday lunch when an urgent voice interrupted their radio program. Japan, the announcer said, had dropped a bomb on Pearl Harbor, Hawaii. No one believed it was true.

With graduation just five months away, Yoshiko thought instead about her final exams at the University of California at Berkeley. She rushed off to the library to study. When Yoshiko returned home that evening, FBI men were in her living room. Her father had been taken for questioning.

Soon after, Yoshiko and her family were forced to leave their Berkeley home. Taken to Tanforan Racetrack Assembly Center, they were confined in a ten-by-twenty-foot horse stall. Without a trial or hearing of any kind, the Uchidas, along with 120,000 other Americans of Japanese ancestry, were to be imprisoned in concentration camps. "How could America—our own country—have done this to us?" wondered Uchida.[1] It was not until many years later that Yoshiko Uchida could bring herself to write about this painful experience.

Dwight and Iku Umegaki Uchida, Yoshiko's parents, were *Issei:* first-generation immigrants from Japan. After arriving in the United States in the early 1900s, the couple were married in Portland, Oregon. They had a daughter, Keiko, and on November 24, 1921, another daughter, Yoshiko, was born. Dwight's business career took the family to the San Francisco Bay area.

In their close-knit Berkeley neighborhood, Yoshiko and her sister, called Kay, enjoyed the simple pleasures of childhood. Best friends lived right next door. The girls made regular trips into San Francisco, where their parents took them to movies, concerts, and art museums.

The written word was important to the Uchida family, and Yoshiko later remembered being surrounded by books at home. Like her mother, Yoshiko kept a diary in which she wrote down her daily thoughts. By the time she was in sixth grade, her little notebooks quickly filled with imaginative stories. At that time it never occurred to her to write about a Japanese American child.

When an earthquake rattled the old building of her local junior high school, Yoshiko was reassigned to Willard Junior High. Although she was nervous about attending an all-white school, Yoshiko made a few good friends, like Sylvia, who invited her to join the Girl Reserves. "Once when our group was to be photographed for the local newspaper . . . ," Uchida wrote, "the photographer casually tried to ease me out of the picture. I knew why, and so did Sylvia. 'Come on, Yoshi,' she said, grabbing my arm. 'Stand next to me.' We linked arms and stood firm."[2] The two friends remained close throughout life.

By high school, Yoshiko was eager to get out, and she graduated in just two and a half years. At age sixteen, she entered the University of California at Berkeley, where she majored in English, philosophy, and history. With other *Nisei* (second-generation Japanese Americans) she enjoyed an active social life and began dating.

"It was during my senior year at Cal . . . that my happy, carefree life came to an abrupt end," said Uchida.[3] By the evening of December 7, 1941, Dwight Uchida had been taken by the FBI. The family left the porch light on for his return.

With the country at war with Japan, Yoshiko's parents were suddenly considered "enemy aliens." By law, at that time, no Asian could become a naturalized U.S. citizen. Simply because they looked like the enemy, Japanese Americans became targets of hatred and suspicion. Anti-Japanese groups began calling

Yoshiko Uchida on the Berkeley campus, in the front row, second from the right.

for the mass removal of Japanese from the West Coast.

Five days after Dwight Uchida was taken, Yoshiko's family learned that he was being held at the Immigration Detention Headquarters in San Francisco. They visited him before he was sent to an army prisoner of war camp in Missoula, Montana. They wondered when they would see him again.

On February 19, 1942, President Roosevelt signed Executive Order 9066, which resulted in the eviction of all Japanese from the West Coast. Years later, in her book *The Bracelet* (1993), Uchida described this experience through the eyes of a seven-year-old girl, Emi. It was crazy, thought Emi. Her family "loved America, but America didn't love them back."[4]

The Uchidas were given ten days to prepare for their removal from Berkeley. Allowed to take only what they could carry, they were forced to sell or give away almost everything, including their beloved dog, Lucky.

The family was sent to Tanforan Racetrack, a temporary "assembly center" in northern California, where they were assigned an "apartment," a small, dark horse stall that smelled of manure. That same year, Yoshiko graduated with honors from Berkeley. Her diploma was delivered in a cardboard tube, addressed to "stall number 40."[5] On May 8, her father was released from Montana. With four cots crowded into the tiny stall, the family was reunited.

After five months at Tanforan, they were transferred to Topaz, Utah, one of ten concentration camps used to intern Japanese Americans. Surrounded by barbed wire and armed guard towers, the ill-equipped camp was a difficult place to live. Inmates waited in long lines at the mess hall and toilets, which often did not work. Entire families lived in single rooms, where thin-walled barracks offered little protection from choking dust storms.

Despite these conditions, inmates tried to rebuild a community. Kay and Yoshiko helped organize the schools. They were determined to see the children continue their education.

One day in the spring of 1943, Yoshiko's father burst into her classroom, waving a piece of paper. Both Yoshiko and Kay had won clearances to leave Topaz. Though it was difficult to leave everyone behind, their parents encouraged the girls to move ahead with their lives. The National Japanese Student Relocation Council, a Quaker organization, awarded Uchida a full scholarship for graduate studies at Smith College in Massachusetts.

At Smith, Yoshiko earned her master's degree in education. Proudly marching with her classmates in a cap and gown, Yoshiko enjoyed the graduation ceremonies she had missed at Berkeley. She then headed to Philadelphia, where she had been hired to teach.

In the summer of 1944, Kay joined her sister in Philadelphia. In their tiny rented apartment they had a joyous reunion with their parents, who were finally free.

Although she enjoyed teaching at the Frankford Friends School, Uchida wanted more time to write. So she moved to New York City and found a nine-to-five job as a secretary. At night and on weekends she wrote. She submitted her stories to magazines and was met with rejections. But then her work started coming back with encouraging notes. One editor urged Yoshiko to write about her concentration camp experiences.

In 1949, Yoshiko published her first book, *The Dancing Kettle*, a collection of Japanese folktales. Her career as a children's writer had begun.

On a Ford Foundation fellowship, Yoshiko took a trip to Japan that changed her life. She discovered the richness of Japanese culture and embraced it as her own: "Slowly, I realized that everything I admired and loved about Japan was a part of me. My parents had been giving it to me, like a gift, every day of my life."[6]

After years of struggling, Yoshiko was finding out who she was. She wanted to share this sense of pride and self-esteem with the third-generation Japanese Americans—the *Sansei*—by writing books about Asian children.

The subjects and stories she had collected in Japan inspired many of her books, including *The Magic Listening Cap* and *The Sea of Gold*. When her eighth book, *Rokubei and the Thousand Rice Bowls*, was published in 1962, Yoshiko had become a full-time writer.

In 1966, her mother's death moved Uchida to write her parents' story. She wanted to give the *Sansei* "a sense of the courage and strength of the first-generation Japanese whose survival over countless hardships was truly a triumph of the human spirit!"[7]

Based on her family's experiences, *Journey to Topaz* follows twelve-year-old Yuki, a second-generation Japanese American girl in Berkeley, and the uprooting of her family after the bombing of Pearl Harbor. Published in 1971 to critical acclaim, *Journey to Topaz* is perhaps Uchida's best-known work and continues to move young readers today. One child wrote that *Topaz* gave her "a sharp pain in my heart."[8]

In 1978 Uchida published *Journey Home*, the sequel to *Topaz*, in which Yuki and her family return to California to rebuild their lives after the war. In the trilogy *A Jar of Dreams* (1981), *The Best Bad Thing* (1983), and *The Happiest Ending* (1985), Uchida created her popular heroine Rinko, who grows up in Depression-era Berkeley. Praised as "genuine and refreshing," spunky Rinko is a Japanese American adolescent all kids can relate to.[9] While Uchida wrote mainly about Japanese subjects, she also said that she wanted her writing to "celebrate our common humanity."[10]

Uchida lived her later years in Berkeley, a short distance from her childhood home. Forty years after the camps, she witnessed the apology of the U.S. government, who acknowledged that a terrible injustice had been done to Japanese Americans as a result of racial prejudice.

Before her death in 1992, Yoshiko Uchida spoke to children about her life and her work. She told them she was angry about how Japanese Americans were treated by the government during World War II. Through her books she hoped to move readers to cherish freedom and democracy so they would not let such a tragedy happen again, to anyone.

Laurence Yep

Laurence Yep
(1948–   )

"I think of myself as an outsider," said Laurence Yep.[1] Today Yep is an award-winning author of books for children and young adults. But when he was growing up, Yep struggled to find his place in the world. He was the only Chinese child in a black neighborhood. He did not speak Chinese, which made him feel like a foreigner in nearby Chinatown. Yet he was too Chinese to fit in anywhere else.

Much of Yep's writing concerns outsiders. Within alien worlds or present-day Chinatown, Yep's characters struggle to find their way, often in the face of prejudice and other challenges.

Laurence Michael Yep was born on June 14, 1948, in San Francisco. Yep's mother, Franche Lee, was born and raised in the Midwest before moving to California. Yep's father, Yep Gim Lew, left China for America at age ten to join his father, a railroad worker. Yep's father and mother met in San Francisco, where they married.

Together with his parents and older brother, Thomas, called Spike, Laurence lived outside Chinatown in an apartment above his parents' grocery store. Early on, Laurence went to work "feeding the beast"—as he called his parents' store—stocking the shelves and doing various other chores.[2] The hard work and daily routine of the store taught Yep the discipline he later used as a writer. Despite their own twelve-hour workdays, his parents still made time for fun, flying fancy kites handmade by his father and taking day trips in Jezebel, their 1939 Chevy.

While his mom, dad, and brother enjoyed athletics, Laurence said he was "lousy at sports."[3] In later years Yep's father took pride in his son's books. In place of athletic trophies, he would display the awards Yep won for his writing.

When Laurence was seven, his world was torn apart. The neighborhood changed and many of his friends moved away. In time, the close-knit neighborhood dissolved.

Growing up in the 1950s was difficult for Laurence; it was a time when everyone was expected to fit in and minorities often faced prejudice. Once, Yep was approached by some kids playing soldier. Finding himself under attack, Yep realized he was being used as the "all-purpose Asian." He could have been Korean, or Japanese; they saw only his Asian features. "It made me feel like an outsider more than ever in my own neighborhood."[4]

Turning to books, Laurence often visited the public library. Books helped him sort things out. "The Oz books [by L. Frank Baum] talked about survival. They dealt with the real mysteries of life—like finding yourself and your place in the world. And that was something I tried to do every day I got on and off the bus."[5]

Books also offered some comfort during Laurence's asthma attacks. During sleepless nights as he sat propped up trying to breathe, his mother read to him. His favorites were science fiction stories, which set his imagination on fire.

Laurence attended St. Mary's grammar school near Chinatown, which later became a Chinese school. There Laurence was placed in what he called "the dummies' class" to learn Chinese, which was not spoken in his household.[6] Laurence stubbornly refused to learn the language.

"At a time when so many children are now proud of their ethnic heritages, I'm ashamed to say that when I was a child, I didn't want to be Chinese," Yep has admitted.[7] He recalls rejecting other symbols of Asianness, from martial arts to chopsticks, which he did not learn to use until age twelve. But when he rode the streetcar into Chinatown to see his grandmother, Marie Lee, Yep could not avoid her "Chineseness."

Despite the language barrier, Marie Lee became a great influence in Laurence's life. Simply by being around her, Yep absorbed Chinese culture, as well as her unique Chinese American identity.

Marie Lee was a strong person who felt at home whether she was in her native China, in Clarksburg, West Virginia, or in San Francisco's Chinatown. In her West Virginia garden his grandmother tended Chinese vegetables. In her kitchen she learned to bake the best apple pies. Seeking balance in his own life, Yep admired how his family and other Chinese Americans lived within two cultures. Yep found himself drawn to their stories, and he started keeping a file of his family history.

In school, Yep's interest in science had him planning a career as a chemist, at one time his father's own dream. But an inspiring English teacher, Father Becker, started him writing stories, and Yep was hooked.

Yep's interest in writing led him to Marquette University, where he entered the journalism program in 1966. When his professor told him that he had more talent for writing fiction than for journalism, Yep became discouraged. However, during this time he met fellow student Joanne Ryder, who encouraged him to write and publish his own work.

Yep sold "The Selchey Kids," his first science fiction story, to a magazine, earning him a penny a word. Laurence liked writing science fiction. However, other stories met with rejection.

Meanwhile, Yep transferred from Marquette, earning a bachelor's degree in 1970 from the University of California at Santa Cruz.

Three years after his first sale, he got a call from Ryder, who was working at the publishing house Harper & Row. She asked him to write a children's story. The result, *Sweetwater*, was published in 1973. In *Sweetwater*, a science fiction novel, young Tyree belongs to an alien minority group struggling for survival on the planet Harmony. Only later did Yep realize that his alien characters faced the same misunderstanding that he had known as a Chinese American.

In his next book, Yep wrote directly about Chinese Americans. *Dragonwings* was published in 1975, the same year Yep received a Ph.D. in English from the State University of New York at Buffalo.

Yep had spent six years researching Chinese American history. He found few details on the early immigrants. During his research, he learned about Chinese American Fung Joe Guey, who built and flew a biplane in 1909, just six years after the Wright brothers' famous flight.

Dragonwings is based on the few published facts of this daring feat. Yep tells the story of Windrider, who comes from China to the Land of the Golden Mountain, America. Together with his eight-year-old son, Moonshadow, Windrider realizes his dream of flying. Chinese folklore and myth are blended with actual events, such as the San Francisco earthquake, the early Chinatown community, and Fung Joe Guey's amazing flight.

Also notable are the book's multidimensional Chinese-American characters. With his writing, Yep has tried to counter the stereotyped negative images of Chinese he had so often seen in literature and the media while he was growing up. *Dragonwings* was named a Newbery Honor Book in 1976.

In 1977, Laurence Yep wrote *Child of the Owl*, in which twelve-year-old Casey Young is sent to live with her grandmother, Paw-Paw, in San Francisco's Chinatown. Casey's personal struggle with her Chinese heritage is based on the experiences of Yep's mother and grandmother.

Imagining his grandmother as a teenager, Yep portrayed rebel Cassia Young and nineteenth-century peasant life in *The Serpent's Children*, published in 1982.

Writers are often advised to write what they know, and Yep has found his personal background to be a rich source. He looked to his own childhood for *Sea Glass*, whose protagonist Craig Chin, awkward and overweight, feels rejected by both white and Chinese worlds. Such self-examination can be painful, and Yep also turns to other subjects.

In the 1980s, Yep created an entire universe with his popular dragon series. The four volumes of this fantasy series—*Dragon of the Lost Sea, Dragon Steel, Dragon Cauldron,* and *Dragon War*—trace the magical adventures of the exiled dragon princess Shimmer

In his writing, Yep creates characters who are outsiders on their own journeys of self-discovery.

and the boy Thorn, who try to restore the dragon homeland, the Inland Sea. Book critics and readers have praised the books for their unique characters, action-packed adventure, and integration of Chinese mythology.

Over time, Yep and Ryder's friendship grew into love, and in 1989 they married. Sadly, that same year, Yep's father died. Yep's autobiography, *The Lost Garden* (1991), touchingly recalls his family and how his childhood memories inspire him.

With other books Laurence Yep has expanded beyond Chinese and science fiction themes—from teenage romance in *Kind Hearts and Gentle Monsters* to suspense novels such as the Chinatown Mystery Series. Yep has also interpreted Chinese folktales in the form of picture books, including *The Khan's Daughter*. In 1994, Yep picked up his second Newbery Honor for *Dragon's Gate*, published in 1993, the second sequel to *The Serpent's Children*.

A full-time writer, Yep enjoys writing in different styles, saying that he finds "new interesting challenges" with each one.[8] With all of his work, Yep understands his audience, many of whom may feel like outsiders themselves. Chinese American children especially, according to writer Maxine Hong Kingston, will recognize themselves in Yep's books, and feel less alone.[9] But "outsiders eventually come to realize who they are," said Yep.[10] Thus his books are fun to read, filled with humor, suspense, action, and fantasy.

In more than forty books, Laurence Yep has transformed mythical worlds and the Chinese American experience into stories that engage young readers across the generations. Along the way, his writing has led the author—like his characters—to understand himself.

Chapter Notes

Preface

1. Amy Tan, "In the Canon for All the Wrong Reasons," *Harper's*, December 1996, p. 30.

2. Laurence Yep, "Writing 'Dragonwings,'" *The Reading Teacher*, January 1977, pp. 359–363.

3. Anne Commire, ed., *Something About the Author* (Detroit: Gale Research, 1990), vol. 58, p. 121.

4. Judith Graham, ed., "Bharati Mukherjee," *Current Biography Yearbook 1992* (New York: H. W. Wilson, 1992), p. 412.

5. Diane Telgen, ed., *Something About the Author* (Detroit: Gale Research, 1993), vol. 73, p. 33.

6. Kingston biography, "Celebrating Women's History," www.gale.com.

7. Kathleen J. Edger, ed., *Contemporary Authors* (Detroit: Gale Research, 1996), vol. 149, p. 246.

8. Tan, pp. 30–31.

Chapter 1. Carlos Bulosan

1. Susan Evangelista, *Carlos Bulosan and His Poetry: A Biography and Anthology* (Seattle: University of Washington Press, 1985), p. 8.

2. Elaine Kim, *Asian American Literature* (Philadelphia: Temple University Press, 1982), p. 53.

3. Christopher Chow, "A Brother Reflects: An Interview with Aurelio Bulosan," *Amerasia Journal*, May 1979, p. 160.

4. E. San Juan, Jr., "Carlos Bulosan," *The American Radical* (London: Routledge, 1994), p. 258.

5. Stanley Kunitz and Howard Haycraft, eds., *Twentieth Century Authors* (New York: H. W. Wilson, 1985), p. 145.

6. Evangelista, p. 13.

7. Jimin Han, "Home of the Brave," *A. Magazine*, January 31, 1996, p. 65.

8. Carlos Bulosan, "I Am Not a Laughing Man," *The Writer*, May 1946, p. 144.

9. Kim, p. 57.

10. William S. Lynch, "Loyalty in Spite of All," *Saturday Review of Literature*, March 9, 1946.

11. San Juan, Jr., p. 253.

Chapter 2. Sook Nyul Choi

1. Diane Telgen, ed., *Something About the Author* (Detroit: Gale Research, 1993), vol. 73, p. 33.

2. Ibid.

3. Sook Nyul Choi, "Questions About Writing," fact sheet supplied by Sook Nyul Choi.

4. Personal interview with Sook Nyul Choi, April 26, 1999.

5. Ibid.

6. Ibid.

7. Shannon Maughhan, Lynda Brill Comerford, et al., "Flying Starts," *Publishers Weekly*, December 20, 1991, pp. 22–23.

8. Choi, "Questions About Writing."

9. Maughhan, pp. 22–23.

10. Ellen Levine, review of *Echoes of the White Giraffe*, *New York Times Book Review*, May 16, 1993, p. 27.

11. Choi, "Questions About Writing."

12. Personal interview with Sook Nyul Choi, April 26, 1999.

13. Bruce McCabe, "Author's Korean Novel Embraces Her Two Homes," *Boston Globe*, December 3, 1991, p. 66.

14. Maughhan, pp. 22–23.

Chapter 3. Maxine Hong Kingston

1. Maxine Hong Kingston, *The Woman Warrior* (New York: Knopf, 1980), p. 165.

2. Kay Bonetti, "An Interview with Maxine Hong Kingston, 1986" in Paul Skenazy and Tera Martin, eds., *Conversations with Maxine Hong Kingston* (Jackson: University Press of Mississippi, 1998), p. 34.

3. Sylvia Brownrigg, "Books: 'Really We're Mostly Yellow' Asian Americans Are Known as the Model Minority," Manchester, England: *The Guardian,* July 18, 1998, p. 8.

4. Gale Group, "Maxine Hong Kingston: Celebrating Women's History," <http://www.galegroup.com/library/resres/womenhst/kingston.htm> (January 25, 2000).

5. Ibid.

6. Kingston, pp. 201–202.

7. Laura E. Skandera-Trombley, ed., *Critical Essays on Maxine Hong Kingston* (New York: G.K. Hall & Co., 1998), p. 91.

8. Margarett Loke, "The Tao Is Up," *New York Times Magazine,* April 30, 1989, p. 28.

9. Kingston, p. 16.

10. Ibid., p. 53.

11. Gale Group.

12. Hazel Rochman, "Against Borders," *The Horn Book,* March/April 1995, p. 148.

13. Paul Skenazy and Tera Martin, eds., *Conversations with Maxine Hong Kingston* (Jackson: University Press of Mississippi, 1998), p. xi.

14. Timothy Pfaff, *New York Times Book Review,* June 15, 1980, pp. 24–26.

15. Skandera-Trombley, p. 224.

16. Skenazy and Martin, p. 71.

17. Ibid., p. 203.

18. Bert Eljera, "Cultural Icon: President Awards National Humanities Medal to Bay Area Author," *Asian Week*, November 5, 1997, p. 11.

Chapter 4. Marie G. Lee

1. Marie G. Lee, "How I Grew," *The ALAN Review*, winter 1995, <http://scholar.lib.vt.edu/ejournals/ALAN/winter95/Leehtml#AboutAuthor> (January 25, 2000).

2. Ibid.

3. *Authors and Artists for Young Adults (AAYA)*, Thomas McMahon, ed. (Detroit: Gale Group, 2000), vol. 32.

4. *Korean Quarterly*, "People to Look Up To: Marie Lee," winter 1997, <http://www.koreanquarterly.org/ISSUE2/marielee.html> (January 25, 2000).

5. *AAYA*.

6. Ibid.

7. Ronald Takaki, *Lives of Notable Asian Americans: Literature and Education* (New York: Chelsea House Publishers, 1996), p. 91.

8. *AAYA*.

9. *Korean Quarterly*.

10. Kathleen J. Egar, ed., *Contemporary Authors*, (Detroit: Gale Research, 1996), vol. 149, p. 246.

11. *Korean Quarterly*.

12. Ibid.

13. Kevin S. Hile, ed., *Something About the Author (SATA)*, (Detroit: Gale Research, 1995), vol. 81, pp. 123–26.

14. Ibid.

15. Ibid.

16. *AAYA*.

17. *ALAN*.

Chapter 5. Bette Bao Lord

1. Dorothy Hoobler and Thomas Hoobler, *The Chinese American Album* (New York: Oxford University Press, 1994), p. 7.

2. Anne Commire, ed., *Something About the Author (SATA),* (Detroit: Gale Research, 1990), vol. 58, p. 121.

3. Barbara Matusow, "Iron and Silk," *The Washingtonian,* January 1997, p. 158.

4. Hoobler and Hoobler, p. 7.

5. *SATA,* p. 122.

6. Kristin McMurran, *People Weekly,* November 23, 1981, p. 93.

7. *SATA,* p. 122.

8. Stella Dong, *Publishers Weekly,* October 30, 1981, p. 11.

9. Susan M. Trosky, ed., *Contemporary Authors, New Revision Series* (Detroit: Gale Research, 1994), vol. 41, p. 276.

10. Catherine Reeve, "Legacies: A Daughter of China Gives Voice to the Spirits of a Tragic Spring," *Chicago Tribune,* June 3, 1990, sec. 6, p. 8.

11. McMurran, p. 93.

12. Daniel Southerland, "The Creative Diplomacy of Bette Bao Lord," *Washington Post,* September 2, 1987, p. D6.

13. Reeve, p. 1.

14. Sybil S. Steinberg, "Fiction—The Middle Heart," *Publishers Weekly,* December 4, 1995, p. 52.

15. Bette Bao Lord, "An Emigrant's Hopes for China," *Newsweek,* March 3, 1997, p. 48.

Chapter 6. Kyoko Mori

1. Kyoko Mori, *Polite Lies* (New York: Henry Holt and Company, 1998), p. 193.

2. Kevin S. Hile, ed., "Kyoko Mori," *Something About the Author (SATA)* (Detroit: Gale Research, 1995), vol. 82, p. 165.

3. Kyoko Mori, *The Dream of Water* (New York: Henry Holt and Company, 1995), p. 98.

4. *SATA*, p. 165.

5. Ballantine, "Kyoko Mori: A Personal Glimpse," <http://www.randomhouse.com/BB/teachers/> (July 15, 1999).

6. Mori, *The Dream of Water*, p. 6.

7. Ibid., p. 33.

8. Ibid., p. 22.

9. Elizabeth Ward, "The Sins of the Father," *Washington Post*, February 19, 1995, p. 8.

10. *SATA*, p. 166.

11. Ballantine.

12. Ibid.

13. Mori, *The Dream of Water*, p. 9.

14. *SATA*, p. 166.

15. Liz Rosenberg, review of *Shizuko's Daughter*, *New York Times Book Review*, August 22, 1993, p. 19.

16. *SATA*, p. 165.

17. Ibid.

18. Jo Sandin, "In the Midwest, a Japanese-American finds her voice," *Milwaukee Journal Sentinel*, n.d., <http://www.isonline.com/news/sunday/books/> (January 25, 1998).

Chapter 7. Bharati Mukherjee

1. Celia McGee, "Fast Track: Foreign Correspondent," *New York*, January 30, 1989, p. 22.

2. Lavina Melwani, "Bharati Mukherjee: Bridging Time and Space," *Little India*, June 30, 1994, p. 55.

3. Patricia Holt, "Mukherjee's Vision of America," *San Francisco Chronicle*, February 17, 1991, p. 1.

4. Reshma Memon Yaqub, "An American Indian," *Chicago Tribune*, October 10, 1993, sec. 5 p. 3.

5. Mike Hale, "Word Traveler Bharati Mukherjee Records Her View of the Contemporary Immigrant," *Chicago Tribune*, January 16, 1994, p. 4.

6. David Armstrong, "An Immigrant Transformed: Author's Own Life Reflected in Critically Acclaimed Epic Novel," *San Francisco Examiner*, October 28, 1993, p. C1.

7. Judith Graham, ed., "Bharati Mukherjee," *Current Biography* (New York: H. W. Wilson, 1992), p. 411.

8. David Mehegan, "Bharati Mukherjee's Sojourn on Unfamiliar Turf," *Boston Globe*, November 8, 1993, p. 33.

9. Julie Winokur, "The Transformation of Bharati Mukherjee," *San Jose Mercury News*, January 30, 1994, p. 6.

10. Judith Graham, ed., "Bharati Mukherjee," *Current Biography Yearbook 1992* (New York: H. W. Wilson, 1992), p. 412.

11. Ibid.

12. Alison Carb, "An Interview with Bharati Mukherjee," *Massachusetts Review*, 1988, pp. 645–654.

13. Hale, p. 4.

14. Sybil Steinberg, "Bharati Mukherjee," *Publishers Weekly*, August 25, 1989, p. 47.

15. Armstrong, p. C1.

16. Hale, p. 4.

17. Donna Seaman, "Adult Fiction—*The Holder of the World* by Bharati Mukherjee," *Booklist*, September 1, 1993, p. 5.

18. Melwani, p. 55.

Chapter 8. Amy Tan

1. Kim Hubbard, "*The Joy Luck Club* Has Brought Writer Amy Tan a Bit of Both," *People Weekly*, April 10, 1989, pp. 149–150.

2. Ibid.

3. Sarah Rosen, "Children's Express," *New York Amsterdam News*, November 12, 1994, p. 24.

4. Patricia Holt, "Amy Tan Hits the Jackpot with Her First Novel," *San Francisco Chronicle*, March 27, 1989, p. C3.

5. George Gurley, "Amy Tan: The Ghosts and the Writer," Knight-Ridder/Tribune News Service, April 22, 1998, p. 42.

6. Hubbard, pp. 149–150.

7. Ibid.

8. David Gates and Dorothy Wang, "A Game of Show Not Tell," *Newsweek*, April 17, 1989, p. 69.

9. Amy Tan, *The Joy Luck Club* (New York: G. P. Putnam Sons, 1989), p. 7.

10. Jeff Chapman and John D. Jorgenson, eds., *Contemporary Authors, New Revision Series* (Detroit: Gale Research, 1996), vol. 54, p. 389.

11. Nahrissa Rush, Customer Reviews, Amazon.com, n.d., <http://www.amazon.com/exec/obidos/ts/book-customer-reviews/0804106304/o/aid=948738238/sr=8-2/102-376/1915-5758401> (January 23, 1999).

12. Kathey Clarey, "Amy Tan's Literary Concerns," *Fresno Bee*, October 5, 1994, p. B1.

Chapter 9. Yoshiko Uchida

1. Yoshiko Uchida, *The Invisible Thread* (Englewood Cliffs, N.J.: Julian Messner, 1991), p. 79.

2. Ibid., p. 55.

3. Ibid., p. 62.

4. Yoshiko Uchida, *The Bracelet* (New York: Philomel Books, 1993), p. 1.

5. Susan Gall, ed., *The Asian American Almanac* (Detroit: Gale Research, Inc., 1995), p. 572.

6. Uchida, *The Invisible Thread,* p. 131.

7. Catherine E. Studier Chang, "Profile: Yoshiko Uchida," *Language Arts,* February 1984, p. 193.

8. Ibid.

9. Ethel L. Heins, review of *A Jar of Dreams, The Horn Book,* December 1981, p. 666.

10. Pamela S. Dear, ed., *Contemporary Authors New Revision Series* (Detroit: Gale Research, 1996), vol. 47, p. 448.

Chapter 10. Laurence Yep

1. Chizu Omori, "Age of Wonders Bring Laurence Yep to Town," *International Examiner,* July 4, 1995, p. 9.

2. Laurence Yep, *The Lost Garden* (Englewood Cliffs, N.J.: Messner, 1991), p. 15.

3. Amy Ehrlich, ed., *When I Was Your Age,* (Cambridge, Mass.: Candlewick Press, 1996), p. 37.

4. Yep, p. 38.

5. Ibid., p. 77.

6. Ibid., p. 52.

7. Ibid., p. 43.

8. Helen Zia and Suan B. Gall, eds., *Asian American Biography* (Detroit: Gale Research, 1995), vol. 2, p. 393.

9. Pamela S. Dear, ed., "Laurence Yep," *Contemporary Authors New Revision Series* (Detroit: Gale Research, 1995), vol. 46, p. 481.

10. Patrick Burnson, "In the Studio with Laurence Yep," *Publishers Weekly,* May 16, 1994, p. 25.

Further Reading

A Selected List

Hoobler, Dorothy and Thomas Hoobler, introduction by Bette Bao Lord. *The Chinese-American Family Album.* New York: Oxford University Press Children's Books, 1998.

Marvis, Barbara J. *Contemporary American Success Stories: Famous People of Asian Ancestry.* Childs, Md.: Mitchell Lane Publishers, 1993.

Takaki, Ronald. *Lives of Notable Asian Americans.* New York: Chelsea House, 1995.

The Asian American Cybernauts Page

A guide to Asian American resources on the Web. Among the categories: organizations by ethnic group, culture, concerns, and a page of Asian American quotes.
<http://janet.org/~ebihara/wataru_aacyber.html>

Asian-American Literature

History, classroom use, bibliography, and Web Resources; a comprehensive resource listing with active links.
<http://falcon.jmu.edu/~ramseyil/asialit.htm>

A. Magazine: Inside Asian America

The Web site of the hip AA magazine, the largest-circulation Asian publication in the United States Articles on Asian pop culture, politics, fashion, prominent Asian Americans, and other current topics.
<http://www.amagazine.com>

Asian Pacific American Resources at the Smithsonian

An overview and links to current Smithsonian resources of particular significance to Asian Pacific Americans. Includes information on museum collections, exhibitions, and educational activities. <http://www.si.edu/resource/tours/asian/start.htm>

South Asian Women Writers

Bibliographies and interviews, with audio clips, of a long list of South Asian authors. Created by Sawnet, the South Asian Women's Network. <http://www.umiacs.umd.edu/users/sawweb/sawnet/books_bios.html#chitra_divakaruni>

• • •

Carlos Bulosan

Chorus for America: Six Filipino Poets. Los Angeles: Wagon and Star, 1942.

Letter from America. Prairie City, Ill.: J. A. Decker, 1942.

The Voice of Bataan. New York: Coward McCann, 1943.

The Laughter of My Father. New York: Harcourt, Brace and Co., 1944.

America Is in the Heart. New York: Harcourt, Brace and Co., 1946; reprinted 1973 by University of Washington Press.

"Revisiting the Life and Legacy of Pioneering Filipinos Writer Carlos Bulosan" <http://www.reflectionsofasia.com/carlosbulosan.htm>

• • •

Sook Nyul Choi

Year of Impossible Goodbyes. Boston: Houghton Mifflin, 1991.

Echoes of the White Giraffe. Boston: Houghton Mifflin, 1993.

Halmoni and the Picnic. Boston: Houghton Mifflin, 1993.

Gathering of Pearls. Boston: Houghton Mifflin, 1994.

The Best Older Sister. New York: Delacorte, 1997.

Yummi and Halmoni's Trip. Boston: Houghton Mifflin, 1997.

"Discovering Sook Nyul Choi's Autobiographical Novels for Young Adults" <http://www.koreanquarterly.org/ISSUE2/revchoi2.html>

• • •

Maxine Hong Kingston

The Woman Warrior: Memoirs of a Girlhood Among Ghosts. New York: Knopf, 1976.

China Men. New York: Knopf, 1980.

Hawaii One Summer. San Francisco: Meadow Press, 1987.

Tripmaster Monkey: His Fake Book. New York: Knopf, 1989.

"Maxine Hong Kingston" <http://encarta.msn.com/index/conciseindex/AB/0AB79000.htm?2=1&pg=2+br=1>

• • •

Marie G. Lee

Finding My Voice. Boston: Houghton Mifflin, 1992.

If It Hadn't Been for Yoon Jun. Boston: Houghton Mifflin, 1993.

Saying Goodbye. Boston: Houghton Mifflin, 1994.

Necessary Roughness. New York: HarperCollins, 1996.

Night of the Chupacabras. New York: Camelot, 1998.

Marie G. Lee's Official Home Page

A brief biography of Lee, with links to the Asian American Writers Workshop, Kimchinet, children's book authors page, and more.
<http://www.geocities.com/Athens/Acropolis/4416/>

• • •

Bette Bao Lord

Eighth Moon: The True Story of a Young Girl's Life in Communist China. New York: Harper, 1964.

Spring Moon: A Novel of China. New York: Harper, 1981.

In the Year of the Boar and Jackie Robinson. New York: Harper, 1984.

Legacies: A Chinese Mosaic. New York: Alfred A. Knopf, 1990.

The Middle Heart. New York: Knopf, 1996.

Fox, Mary Virginia. *Bette Bao Lord: Novelist and Chinese Voice for Change.* Danbury, Conn.: Children's Press, 1993.

"Bette Bao Lord: Booknotes Interview"
<http://www.booknotes.org/transcripts/50013.htm>

• • •

Kyoko Mori

Shizuko's Daughter. New York: Henry Holt, 1993.

Fallout. Chicago: TiaChucha Press, 1994.

The Dream of Water: A Memoir. New York: Henry Holt, 1995.

One Bird. New York: Henry Holt, 1995.

Polite Lies. New York: Henry Holt, 1998.

"Kyoko Mori: A Personal Glimpse"
<http://www.randomhouse.com/BB/teachers/bios/mori.html>

• • •

Bharati Mukherjee

Wife. Boston: Houghton Mifflin, 1975.

Days and Nights in Calcutta. New York: Doubleday, 1977.

The Middleman and Other Stories. New York: Grove, 1988.

Jasmine. New York: Grove, 1989.

The Holder of the World. New York: Knopf, 1993.

Leave It to Me. New York: Knopf, 1997.

Alam, Fakrul. *Bharati Mukherjee.* Twayne's United States Authors, 653, Twayne Publishers, 1995.

"American Dreamer," a biographical article by Mukherjee <http://www.mojones.com/mother_jones/JF97/mukherjee.html>

• • •

Amy Tan

The Joy Luck Club. New York: Putnam, 1989.

The Kitchen God's Wife. New York: Putnam, 1991.

The Moon Lady. New York: Macmillan, 1992.

The Chinese Siamese Cat. New York: Macmillan, 1994.

The Hundred Secret Senses. New York: Putnam, 1995.

Kramer, Barbara. *Amy Tan: Author of the* Joy Luck Club. Berkeley Heights, N.J.: Enslow Publishers, 1996.

Anniina's Amy Tan Page

Everything Amy! A dedicated fan created this site, which includes book reviews, an interview with video clips, an Amy Tan Quiz, and a schedule of Tan's upcoming appearances. <http://www.luminarium.org/contemporary/amytan/index.html>

• • •

Yoshiko Uchida

Journey to Topaz. New York: Scribner, 1971.

Samurai of Gold Hill. New York: Scribner, 1972.

Journey Home. New York: McElderry Books, 1978.

A Jar of Dreams. New York: McElderry Books, 1981.

Desert Exile. Seattle: University of Washington Press, 1982.

The Best Bad Thing. New York: McElderry Books, 1983.

The Happiest Ending. New York: McElderry Books, 1985.

Picture Bride. Cadillac, Mich.: Northland Press, 1987.

The Bracelet. New York: Philomel, 1993.

The Invisible Thread. Englewood Cliffs, N.J.: Julian Messner, 1991, reprinted Beech Tree, 1995.

• • •

Laurence Yep

Dragonwings. New York: Harper & Row, 1975.

Child of the Owl. New York: Harper & Row, 1977.

Dragon of the Lost Sea. New York: Harper & Row, 1982.

The Mark Twain Murders. Four Winds Press, 1982.

The Serpent's Children. New York: Harper & Row, 1982.

Dragon Steel. New York: Harper & Row, 1985.

Mountain Light. New York: Harper & Row, 1985.

The Star Fisher. New York: Morrow, 1991.

The Lost Garden. Englewood Cliffs, N.J.: Julian Messner, 1991.

Dragon War. New York: HarperCollins, 1992.

Dragon's Gate. New York: HarperCollins, 1993.

American Dragons: Twenty-Five Asian American Voices. New York: HarperCollins, 1993.

Ghost Fox. New York: Scholastic, 1994.

Hiroshima. New York: Scholastic, 1995.

Later, Gator. New York: Hyperion Books for Children, 1995.

Thief of Hearts. New York: HarperCollins, 1995.

The Case of the Goblin Pearls (The Chinatown Mystery Series No. 1). New York: HarperCollins, 1997.

The Case of the Lion Dance (The Chinatown Mystery Series No. 2). New York: HarperCollins, 1998.

The Imp That Ate My Homework. New York: HarperCollins, 1998.

The Cook's Family. New York: Putnam, 1998.

The Amah. New York: Putnam, 1999.

Johnson-Feelings, Dianne. *Presenting Laurence Yep.* Twayne's United States Authors, 656, Boston: Twayne Publishers, 1995.

Laurence Yep Web Page
Children's author Links from the Internet School Library Media Center.

A good starting point for researching a host of authors, with a biography and book reviews, Yep lesson plans, and a teacher's cyber guide to *Dragonwings.*

<http://falcon.jmu.edu/~ramseyil/yep.htm>

Index

Page numbers for photographs are in **boldface** type.